IMAGES
of America

HOLLYWOOD
1940–2008

HOLLYWOOD BOULEVARD AT NIGHT, 1963. Hollywood Boulevard has always been the center of Hollywood premieres. Hollywood Boulevard and Vine Street were historically known as the "Downtown" of Hollywood, where large gatherings for special events occurred year after year. (Courtesy of Bison Archives.)

ON THE COVER: Grauman's Chinese Theatre is seen in 1953 during the premiere of *The Robe*. Hollywood Boulevard became world famous for premieres, which would draw glamorous celebrities who were publicizing Hollywood films.

IMAGES
of America

HOLLYWOOD
1940–2008

Marc Wanamaker

ARCADIA
PUBLISHING

Published by Arcadia Publishing
Charleston, South Carolina

Library of Congress Catalog Card Number: 2008926396

For all general information contact Arcadia Publishing at:
Telephone 843-853-2070
Fax 843-853-0044
E-mail sales@arcadiapublishing.com
For customer service and orders:
Toll-Free 1-888-313-2665

Visit us on the Internet at www.arcadiapublishing.com

SUNSET BOULEVARD AND VINE STREET TRAFFIC LIGHT, 1940. Hollywood traffic lights and street signs were often used to publicize Hollywood in articles and advertisements.

CONTENTS

ACKNOWLEDGMENTS

Volume 2 of the Hollywood saga combines information and photographs from both Bison Archives and the Hollywood Heritage Museum's collection. Many of the contemporary photographs were taken by the author, who has been documenting Los Angeles for three decades.

The author created Bison Archives in 1971 during research for an encyclopedic history of American film studios. The archive is composed of studio photographs and research materials collected since 1970. Bison Archives is more of a research library than a stock photograph archive. The author joined Hollywood Heritage in 1983 when the Lasky-DeMille Barn was acquired for preservation, then reopened as a Hollywood museum. A main driving force in Hollywood Heritage and Hollywood preservation has been Robert W. Nudelman.

This book is dedicated to Mr. Nudelman, whose drive and leadership will be greatly missed. He passed away in May 2008. Once envisioned as a coauthor of this book, he is now not only its dedicatee, but also part of its story (see the introduction and chapter 10). He worked tirelessly toward preserving Hollywood's past.

The Hollywood Heritage Museum Archive has benefited through the generosity of friends and strangers. Thanks go to the following people at Hollywood Heritage: Richard Adkins, Robert S. Birchard, John Clifford, Phil Dockter, Marian Gibbons, Randy Haberkamp, Christy McAvoy, Fran Offenhauser, Marvin Paige, Arnold Schwartzman, Thad Smith, Kay Tornborg, Delmar Watson, and Valerie Yaros.

Major support has come from Jaime Rigler, Cecilia DeMille Presley, the late Charlton Heston, Sharon and Ray Courts, Paramount Pictures, 20th Century Fox Studios, History for Hire, Mann Theaters, Hollywood Pantages Theater, Claire Bradford, Veronica Chavez, Jim Craig, Catherine Patterson Davis, the late Johnny Grant and the Hollywood Historic Trust, Amy Higgins, Eugene L. Hilchey, Betty Lasky, the late Julian "Bud" Lesser, Grant Loucks, Portland Mason, Ruth and Sol Nudelman, Rica and Randy Van Ausdell, Ken Annakin, Pat Hitchcock, Carla Laemmle, the late Jan Sterling, Rod Taylor, the late Henry Wilcoxon, Jonathan Winters, Robert Wise, Robert Cushman of the Academy of Motion Picture Arts and Sciences, Dan Schwartz, and Michael York. Other contributors to this book include Joel Tator, Mike Hawks, Jeff Mantor, and the late Peter Bateman—all from Larry Edmunds Bookshop—and Michael Peter Yakaitis of the Library of Moving Images, Michael Goodrow, and Eugene Edelman of Bison Productions.

INTRODUCTION

This volume is the second of a pair, beginning with *Early Hollywood*. The first volume dealt with Hollywood from the post-rancho period of the 1880s and the development of the Hollywood area into the 20th century. The years beginning with 1940 show Hollywood's incredible development from a small farming community to a major Los Angeles landmark. In only 50 years, the Hollywood area was completely changed into a major business and residential community.

By 1940, Hollywood was going through another boom with the remodeling of many of the old restaurants, theaters, hotels, and apartment houses. The State of California decided to build the Hollywood Parkway, which later became the Hollywood Freeway, in 1954. By 1940, the Sunset Strip was also expanding and was becoming a place of dining entertainment rivaling the nightclubs of Hollywood proper with the opening of Ciro's, the newest of the Hollywood nightclubs at that time.

With the coming of World War II, Hollywood was busier than ever as the studios churned out films by the hundreds created by thousands of employees serviced by the hundreds of businesses and publicity the town generated. The Hollywood Canteen, where servicemen were entertained, became world famous, resulting in a motion picture of the same name. It was at this time that many of Hollywood's original farm and residential landmarks disappeared and were replaced by new public and private buildings changing the look of the town.

With the coming of the 1950s, television emerged as a major entertainment and communication force, and specialized studios were constructed. The Hollywood theaters remodeled as they adapted to the competition with new wide-screen motion pictures. In 1954, the Capitol Records building became one of the newest Hollywood landmarks. The Lasky-DeMille Barn, located on the Paramount Pictures back lot, became a California Historic State Landmark on December 27, 1956. The following year, the Hollywood Hotel was demolished to make way for a bank building, part of the new Hollywood development of the 1950s.

Hollywood lost many original landmarks throughout the 1960s and 1970s. The Hollywood Library burned, and many of the famed restaurants and nightclubs disappeared, such as the Hollywood Brown Derby and the famed Tiny Naylor's Drive-In. But new Hollywood landmarks also were born with the opening of the Cinerama Dome Theater and the RCA Building. The old Moulin Rouge Theater, formerly the Earl Carroll Theater, became the rock 'n' roll venue the Kaleidoscope in 1968. In 1972, Columbia Pictures Studios moved out of Hollywood, and later become a rental studio where television production dominated.

The Pantages opened as a legitimate theater in 1977 in an attempt to bring the tourists toward the eastern end of the boulevard. In the 1980s and 1990s, several plans to rejuvenate Hollywood were met with success and failure. The greatest set back came with the 1994 Northridge earthquake, which severely damaged many buildings in Hollywood, including the historic Egyptian Theatre. In 1997, the most important redevelopment project took shape in the Hollywood-Highland project, which became a shopping and restaurant mall with the Kodak-Academy Awards Theater set in the center. Opening in 1998, the project that encompassed the Renaissance Hotel began a major redevelopment that continued into the next decade.

HOLLYWOOD HERITAGE AND ROBERT W. NUDELMAN

The late Robert W. Nudelman spent much of his time searching for memorabilia to create a unique archive for Hollywood Heritage. Most of the photographs and other printed memorabilia were acquired from various sources on a daily basis for several years. This book is dedicated to the longtime tenacity of Robert in finding Hollywood historical artifacts, whether they were photographs, books, costumes, or a 1,000-pound theater marquee sign. Hollywood Heritage Museum is indebted to Mr. Nudelman for creating a unique archive for future study and for leading efforts to preserve Hollywood's historic landmarks.

After the devastating fire at the Hollywood Library, the Hollywood Heritage Museum Archive began to acquire museum-quality artifacts and materials for research and study. The "Barn" was moved to its current site in 1983 and opened on December 13, 1985, with a small but important collection.

By 1996, the museum's archive numbered about 500 items. After a September 1996 arson fire, the museum took a new approach under Nudelman, locating and acquiring materials related to the Hollywood community's history, early filmmaking, and Paramount Pictures. Within 10 years, over 12,000 items were in the archive, where they were preserved and catalogued for museum displays and research.

HOLLYWOODLAND SIGN, 1941. The famous Hollywood sign at this time still read, "Hollywoodland," which originally was an advertisement for the largest housing development in Hollywood's history, in 1923. With the introduction of television to Los Angeles, Don Lee's KHJ television station was the first to have its transmitter located on the top of Mount Hollywood, in 1939. Los Angeles renamed the hill Mount Lee.

One

HOLLYWOOD PICTORIAL

Hollywood transformed after the Great Depression with the help of the motion picture and radio industries. People were streaming to Los Angeles from around the world looking for work in the entertainment industries, thus, fueling development. Housing, entertainment, and business services thrived, changing the physical landscape and creating new landmarks.

The Hollywood Brown Derby remained the leading restaurant. Retail stores in the area boomed during the radio days, making Hollywood a shopping destination to rival downtown Los Angeles and Beverly Hills. The nightlife in Hollywood expanded with the addition of the Hollywood Palladium and Ciro's, among others. Record companies expanded recording studios, and many musicians worked in the industry supplying music for the movies, radio, and records and supplying live performances at the many bars, clubs, auditoriums, and theaters.

With the coming of World War II, soldiers passed through town 24 hours a day. The war saved many Hollywood nightclubs and rejuvenated others, and kept the hotels at a high capacity. Some historic theaters became radio theaters and legitimate theaters were transformed into cinemas.

The studios experienced great growth during the war years, bringing more jobs. The Academy Awards returned to Hollywood in March 1944, increasing their popularity through radio broadcasts. At the war's end, television was already becoming the dominant industry in Hollywood, with radio continuing to supply entertainment nationally. Many thousands of ex-servicemen settled in Los Angeles, changing population demographics and resulting in a new boom.

Hollywood changed again in the 1950s with new housing, businesses, and infrastructures, including the Hollywood Freeway, which dramatically bisected the famous landscape. In 1954, Capitol Records built the first circular office tower in Hollywood, creating an enduring landmark that remains world famous. New television studios were built, such as CBS Television City, and some older theaters were remodeled, trading historic designs for something modern.

Development came to an abrupt halt by 1968; when Hollywood declined, rock 'n' roll transformed Sunset Strip into a music scene, and tourism generally flagged even as Universal Studios and Disneyland were major draws. Some industry support services closed, and Hollywood Boulevard showed that negative effect with empty businesses. Revitalization in the 1980s and 1990s meant both restoration and disappearance for various landmarks.

SUNSET BOULEVARD AND VINE STREET, 1949. By 1949, NBC Radio Studios were located on the northeast corner of Sunset Boulevard and Vine Street. At Selma Avenue and Vine Street, the site of the old Lasky-DeMille Barn, which later was the first Hollywood studio of Paramount Pictures, became a lighting company. Other historic sites on Vine Street included the Hollywood Rooftop Ballroom, Hollywood Brown Derby, Plaza Hotel, It Café, ABC Radio Studios, and Tom Breneman's "Breakfast in Hollywood" club.

SUNSET BOULEVARD AND GOWER STREET, 1940. Taken from the roof of Columbia Square, looking southeast, this photograph shows the area that was once named "Poverty Row" and was later dominated by Columbia Studios. Poverty Row was an area consisting of small film production companies of the first and second decades of the 20th century, including Chadwick, CBC (Cohn-Brandt-Cohn, the precursor of Columbia Studios), Horsley, Francis Ford, Reliable, C. C. Burr, and the Grand studios.

SANTA CLAUS LANE PARADE, 1949.
A Christmas tradition, this parade
was established in 1928 and was
usually hosted by a celebrity grand
marshal. The caption on the original
photograph read, "With all its glimmer
and glamour, Hollywood officially
welcomed Santa Claus last night as
his float crossed Hollywood and Vine.
Aboard the float was Eddie Cantor
and his grandchild, who helped
in staging."

**HOLLYWOOD BOULEVARD
DECORATIONS, 1940.** Businessman
Harry Blaine conceived the idea of
decorating Hollywood Boulevard for
the holidays in 1928. He declared
Hollywood Boulevard as "Santa
Claus Lane," and the opening of the
shopping season was the parade, with
a live reindeer pulling a wheeled sleigh
with Santa and a celebrity.

CHRISTMAS ON HOLLYWOOD BOULEVARD, 1947. The Grauman's Chinese Theatre showed *Daisy Kenyon*, which starred Joan Crawford and Henry Fonda, during the Christmas season.

HOLLYWOOD BOULEVARD AT WILCOX AVENUE, 1944. Located on the northeast corner was the Warners Hollywood Theater, which opened in 1928 with *The Glorious Betsy*, starring Dolores Costello and Conrad Nagel. The stores in the theater building were of the highest quality throughout the 1940s and 1950s.

SUNSET AND CAHUENGA BOULEVARDS, 1949. Cahuenga Boulevard is seen with Ivar Street on the right and Sunset Boulevard at the bottom. The Roberts Drive-In restaurant was prominently situated on Sunset Boulevard on the one of the most traveled streets in Hollywood. At this time, the Hollywood sign has lost its "H" and could be read as "ollywoodland."

IVAR AND YUCCA STREETS, 1940. Looking south on Ivar Street, the scene takes in the famous Van de Kamp bakery windmill store, a landmark for 30 years before being replaced by a restaurant. Down Ivar Street, the Hotel Knickerbocker, built in 1923, was one of Hollywood's most important hotels—until the Hollywood Roosevelt opened in 1927.

OFFICIAL OPENING OF HOLLYWOOD FREEWAY, 1954. Bob Hope was the master of ceremonies in April 1954. The Hollywood Freeway connected downtown Los Angeles to the San Fernando Valley, cutting travel time in half, bisecting Hollywood, and resulting in increases in commerce and population.

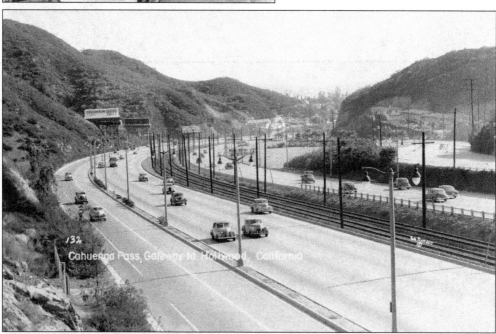

CAHUENGA PASS, 1949. California State Highway 101 was a direct connection from downtown Los Angeles to the San Fernando Valley. The Cahuenga Pass road was originally known as "the Old Pass Road." By 1940, the state began construction of the Hollywood Parkway, with three lanes in each direction. The first phase of the modernization of the freeway was in 1947, adding lanes, but by the 1950s, they expanded the construction program to build a modern freeway over the 1947 work.

HOLLYWOOD POLICE STATION No. 6, 1974. Opened in 1931 at 1358 North Wilcox Avenue, the Hollywood police division of the Los Angeles Police Department expanded due to various community problems in the late 1960s and 1970s. The Hollywood station became known as the "West Bureau," and its officers patrolled 17.2 square miles in the Hollywood district.

HOLLYWOOD ENGINE COMPANY No. 27, TRUCK COMPANY No. 9, 1944. A Columbia Studios publicity photograph shows five-year-old Cheryl Archer, who appeared in the Columbia Studios film *Cover Girl*, visiting the Hollywood Fire Department. The caption reads, "In honor of fire prevention week, Cheryl Archer the youngest of the cover girls appearing in the musical, *Cover Girl*, was appointed honorary fire chief of Los Angeles."

HOLLYWOOD POST OFFICE, 1951. Located at 1615 North Wilcox Avenue, the U.S. Post Office building was constructed in 1936. Designed by Claude Beelman and constructed by Allison and Allison Company, the building is classical moderne in style. At the northern end of the main corridor is *The Pony Express*, a decorative relief depicting two horses and a stagecoach driver carved on mahogany by Gordon Newell of the Federal Art Project.

HOLLYWOOD BOULEVARD AT ORANGE DRIVE, 1952. U.S. Army soldiers climb onto a Pacific Electric trolley car in front of Grauman's Chinese Theatre. Marlon Brando's *Viva Zapata!* was playing at the theater, where Hollywood premieres still dominated the boulevard.

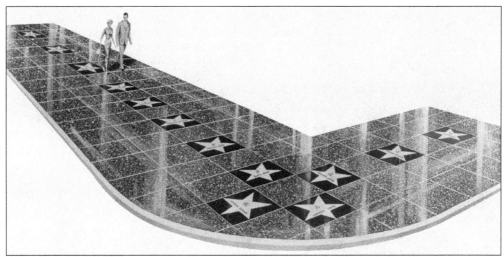

HOLLYWOOD WALK OF FAME MODEL, 1957. The Hollywood Chamber of Commerce spearheaded a glamorization program for Hollywood Boulevard in 1956. One of the major plans was to create an area called "Walk of Fame" that would pay tribute to the artists who made Hollywood famous. The plan called for terrazzo stars to be embedded in the sidewalks of the boulevard and some side streets.

WALK OF FAME STREETLIGHTS, 1958. A new street-lighting system was installed to illuminate the stars on Hollywood Boulevard. From left to right are Hollywood celebrities Antonio Moreno and George Jessel; a Westinghouse street-lighting representative; Harry M. Sugarman of the Hollywood Boulevard Improvement Association, which sponsored the Walk of Fame; actress Marsha Hunt, and actor Gilbert Roland.

HOLLYWOOD WALK OF FAME, 1965. The first eight stars of the Walk of Fame were dedicated in September 1958, placed on the northwest corner of Hollywood Boulevard and Highland Avenue. They were installed months prior to the opening of the 12-story First Federal Savings of Hollywood Building in January 1959. The first artists represented in the sidewalk were Preston Foster, Joanne Woodward, Ernest Torrence, Olive Borden, Edward Sedgwick, Louise Fazenda, Ronald Colman, and Burt Lancaster.

HOLLYWOOD BOULEVARD AND VINE STREET TIME CAPSULE, 1956. Producer Jesse Lasky places Hollywood memorabilia in a time capsule with actress Dorothy Lamour to inaugurate the first phase of Hollywood's glamorization program. The capsule contained the megaphone that C. B. DeMille used in directing *The Squaw Man*, Hollywood's first feature film, as well as Will Rogers's lariat, Bing Crosby's pipe and his gold record of the millionth recording of "Silent Night," Jimmy Durante's hat, Harold Lloyd's glasses, and a revolver used by John Wayne.

HOLLYWOOD BOULEVARD AND VINE STREET, 1959. One of the newer landmarks, the Capitol Records Building opened in April 1956 near this world-famous intersection. Hody's Restaurant was located on the northwest corner of Hollywood Boulevard and Vine Street in the old Laemmle Building, which once housed several other eateries, such as Coco Tree Inn, Melody Lane, and, by the 1980s, Howard Johnson's.

HOLLYWOOD SIGN, 1960. The most famous sign in the world became synonymous with Hollywood and has served as a symbol of the entertainment industry worldwide. By 1978, the sign was in danger of collapsing. The Hollywood Chamber of Commerce organized a multimedia campaign to save it. Celebrities headed by *Playboy* publisher Hugh Hefner donated funds for a new sign, which was unveiled on November 11, 1978.

LAKE HOLLYWOOD, 1959. Located in the hills above Wilcox Avenue, the lake's dam was reinforced after the devastating St. Francis Dam disaster in Santa Clarita in 1928. William Mullholand ordered the front of the dam to be supported by earth, with trees covering the dam's face to allay fears. A true treasure, Lake Hollywood continues to be a City of Los Angeles water reservoir under Cahuenga Peak, near the Hollywood sign.

HOLLYWOOD MEMORIAL PARK CEMETERY, 1959. The DeMille family plot is where famed film director and cofounder of Paramount Pictures Cecil B. DeMille is buried. Along with him are several family members, including his wife, Constance; his brother, William and William's wife, Clara; his mother, Matilda Beatrice DeMille; and his daughter, Cecilia. Cecil B. DeMille died in January 1959.

FIRST FEDERAL BANK BUILDING, 1979. When this photograph was taken, the bank name had been changed to Pacific Federal Bank. Developer C. E. Toberman built the bank on the site of the old Hollywood Hotel. The cornerstone ceremony for the 13-story building was held in January 1957, and Toberman finished the project on February 23, 1959. The building was demolished four decades later for the Hollywood-Highland project.

SUNSET BOULEVARD AT CAHUENGA BOULEVARD, 1963. Looking east along Sunset Boulevard, the Sunset Vine Tower dominates the center of this photograph. At left is the RCA Building under construction, and diagonally across the street at Ivar Street is the construction site of the future Cinerama Dome Theater. Note at the right next to Hoffman TV is one of the locations of *Variety*, a daily and weekly publication about the entertainment industry.

HOLLYWOOD CITIZEN-NEWS BUILDING, 1968. A Columbia Studios film crew is seen on location on Wilcox Avenue. Filming has always been a familiar sight in Hollywood. The Hollywood Citizen-News Building was constructed in 1930 at 1545 Wilcox Avenue to house the first *Hollywood Citizen-News* until 1948, when the company was sold and became the *Citizen News*. This company lasted until 1968, when it was sold and renamed the *Hollywood Citizen-News* before closing its doors in 1970.

HOLLYWOOD REGIONAL BRANCH LIBRARY, 1985. The Frances Howard Goldwyn Library at 1623 North Ivar Street was designed by Frank Gehry in 1985 after a devastating fire in 1983 that destroyed the former library and most of its collections. The Sam Goldwyn Foundation donated the funds to rebuild the library in the name of Goldwyn's wife, Frances. The Special Collections Room was established in 1985 to rebuild the former archives that were lost.

HOLLYWOOD LANDMARKS, 2002. The Capitol Records Building on Vine Street and the KFWB Radio Studios on Argyle Avenue are two of the more important historic entertainment company landmarks. In 2008, development plans for the Capitol Records Building called for it to be remodeled into condo units, and the KFWB building would stand abandoned after the station moved to the Wilshire District of Los Angeles.

MELROSE AND VAN NESS AVENUES, 1941. This westward view on Melrose Avenue takes in two Hollywood landmarks—the Melvan Theater (left) and the Western Costume Company building on the right. Both disappeared in redevelopment projects by Raleigh and Paramount Studios. The Melvan at 5308 Melrose Avenue was renamed the KTLA Studio Television Theater in the late 1940s and later became the Encore Theater in 1963. It was removed to make way for an administration building and sound stage.

HOLLYWOOD BOULEVARD AND VERMONT AVENUE, 1949. Looking north up Vermont Avenue, this view encompasses the Security-First National Bank that stood on the northwest corner and was a landmark for decades in East Hollywood. Up the street on the left was the Studio Theatre, where Laurence Olivier's *Henry V* was playing. Across the street was the famous Sarno's Restaurant, where the waiters sang opera.

LARCHMONT AND BEVERLY BOULEVARDS, 1964. On Hollywood's southern border, Larchmont Village incorporates the area consisting of Hancock Park and Windsor Square. The Larchmont shopping district begins at Melrose Avenue to the north and Third Street to the south. Larchmont was established along the streetcar route servicing Greater Hollywood before 1920 and has maintained popularity as a shopping destination.

Two

PARKS AND RECREATION

Hollywood recreation by 1940 encompassed the movies, radio, and nightclubbing. Residents also went to the beach, Griffith Park, bowling alleys, and enjoyed other sports activities, such as baseball, football, tennis, golf, horseback riding, swimming, polo, and flying. Los Angeles offered all of the above and created historic venues for just about everything recreational.

On the eve of World War II, California State Highway 101 was converted to a freeway that replaced the Old Pass Road through Cahuenga Pass. People loved their cars and traveled to Southern California for recreation. In 1939, the Hollywood Stars baseball club played its games at the newly opened Gilmore Field and Stadium, which hosted football games, while the Pan Pacific Auditorium hosted ice, auto, and horse shows among many other types of large-scale exhibitions.

Hollywood had its own Legion Stadium where one could see movie stars watching prizefights. In 1922, the Hollywood American Legion Post constructed an outdoor boxing arena, and later enclosed it with a heating system for winter fights. The stadium became a part of Hollywood history, but was demolished in the 1960s to make way for a bowling alley. Zoos included Monkey Island, a private attraction surrounded by a moat. The largest zoo was in Griffith Park; it expanded because other smaller Los Angeles attractions closed and the animals were moved there. The Griffith Park Observatory became one of the most prominent Hollywood landmarks and was recently restored, renovated, and enlarged. Griffith Park was the golfing destination for those who wanted to play on a course that once hosted the Los Angeles Open. For the children, Griffith Park has a merry-go-round and Travel Town, which has locomotives as well as a miniature riding train, attractions popular to this day.

The Hollywood Recreation Center on Vine Street had a large bowling alley as its major attraction. The old Warner Brothers Studio on Sunset Boulevard and Bronson Avenue became the Sunset Bowling Center, with 52 lanes and studio teams as rivals. The Hollywood YMCA and Hollywood Athletic Club contained indoor swimming pools and gyms.

HOLLYWOOD LEGION STADIUM, 1940. The Hollywood American Legion Post, organized in 1919, bought property near the corner of Selma and El Centro Avenues. The post constructed an outdoor boxing arena that had wooden bleachers in 1922, and, by 1923, the venue's 6,000 seats were enclosed and heated. For 30-plus years, Hollywood Legion Stadium was a landmark, catering to regulars Mae West, Charles Chaplin, Clark Gable, Humphrey Bogart, Wallace Beery, Errol Flynn, the Three Stooges, and even Claudette Colbert.

MONKEY ISLAND, 1940. Located at 3300 Cahuenga Boulevard, Monkey Island was an independent zoo that was innovatively designed to allow unobstructed views of the monkey and ape habitats surrounded by a moat. Established in Cahuenga Pass around 1937, the attraction was designed so the viewer could see primates huddled together at miniature waterfalls, caves, and ponds. One of the orangutans was Jiggs, an animal movie actor. The owner was Adolph Weiss.

GRIFFITH PARK ZOO, 1940. The newly opened lion habitat was built along with six others in 1939. The cage-less, moat-fronted pits for lions and bears and the 10-cage house for monkeys were constructed. This forerunner to the Los Angeles Zoo was well-stocked with birds, small animals, and herbivores. There was only one elephant at this time and, by 1940, more animals were acquired. Many animals were transferred from the old Selig Zoo at Lincoln Park.

DE LONGPRE PARK, 1940. The Rudolph Valentino Memorial at De Longpre Park was dedicated in 1930 and titled, "Aspiration." Designed by sculptor Roger Noble Burnham, the plaque reads, "Erected in memory of Rudolph Valentino 1895–1926 and presented by his friends and admirers from every walk of life in all parts of the world. In appreciation of the happiness he brought to them by the way of the motion picture."

HOLLYWOOD RECREATION CENTER, 1944. This streamline moderne–style building opened in 1935 at 1539 Vine Street and was first a bowling alley. It was remodeled into Tom Breneman's "Breakfast In Hollywood" Radio Restaurant by 1947. Two years later, it became the radio studios of the American Broadcasting Company (ABC). At the time of this photograph, businesses included Cast Le's Camera Store, Sporting Goods, Broder Clothes, and the Radio Room Nightclub. Later it became Sy Devore, a famous men's clothing store.

HOLLYWOOD YMCA, 1944. This beautiful Spanish Colonial building, located on the southwest corner of Selma and Hudson Avenues, was dedicated on February 19, 1923, by the general secretary of the YMCA, Harry F. Henderson. The property was purchased in 1914. The YMCA maintained a presence in Hollywood with celebrities playing tennis on their courts at nearby Cassil Place. The building contained a gym, plunge, and locker and game rooms. A total renovation was completed in 1995.

GRIFFITH OBSERVATORY, 1949. One of the most popular tourist destinations in Los Angeles was built in 1935, designed by John C. Austin and Frederic M. Ashley in the art deco style with four sciences in mind: astronomy, physics, chemistry, and geology. The 500-seat theater has been presenting planetarium programs for generations and has attracted thousands from around the world. Griffith Observatory has been a frequent filming location, memorably for *Rebel Without A Cause* starring James Dean in 1955.

GILMORE ISLAND, 1950. The Gilmore family struck oil at the beginning of the 20th century and later developed their property into a sports, shopping, and entertainment "island." The Gilmores established the Pan Pacific Auditorium (top left), the Farmers Market (bottom right), Gilmore Drive-In Theater (top right), Gilmore Stadium in 1934 (bottom center), and the Aviation Museum in 1949 (center left). Gilmore Field (center) became the home of the Hollywood Stars baseball team. Years later, CBS Television City was built on the site located at Beverly Boulevard and Fairfax Avenue.

SUNSET BOWLING CENTER, 1946. Opened in 1938, this center was located in a main stage behind the administration building of the old Warner Sunset Studios at 5842 Sunset Boulevard. After the Warner company moved to a larger studio in Burbank in 1928, the Sunset Studio became an annex for the *Looney Tunes* unit. Leon Schlesinger's Warners Brothers cartoon unit was based on the lot from 1930 to 1969.

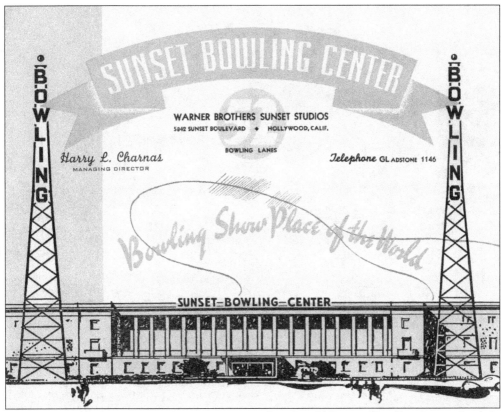

SUNSET BOWLING CENTER MENU, 1955. Located at the old Warner Brothers Sunset Studios, the Sunset Bowling Center became a popular social spot for studio employees involved in bowling leagues. The Warner Brothers Studio Club made the Sunset Bowl their hangout for many years, holding events of all kinds and attracting Hollywood celebrities to make the Sunset Bowling Center the "Bowling Show Place of the World."

FARMERS MARKET, 1950. The Gilmore family purchased two large ranches in the late 19th century in the Hollywood area and created a successful dairy farm. Shortly thereafter, oil was discovered on the property and, by 1905, the Gilmore Oil Company was born. In 1934, entrepreneurs Roger Dahlhjelm and Fred Beck conceived a Village Square on the southwestern section at Fairfax Avenue and Third Street, where artisans would sell handmade goods and farmers their produce.

GRIFFITH PARK CLUBHOUSE AND COURSES, 1940. As part of the old Rancho Los Feliz, Griffith Park was bequeathed to the City of Los Angeles in 1896 by Griffith J. Griffith as a gift for recreational purposes. Parts of the property were developed for recreation, including Griffith Observatory, Greek Theater, Griffith Park Zoo, and the golf courses. The Woodrow Wilson Golf Course opened in 1923 at 4730 Crystal Springs Drive, and the Warren G. Harding Golf Course opened the following year. Both courses hosted the 1937, 1938, and 1939 Los Angeles Open Golf Tournaments.

WILSON AND HARDING MUNICIPAL GOLF COURSES, 1940. Looking west on the San Fernando Valley side of Griffith Park, the Wilson and Harding golf clubhouse is nestled in the foothills (seen top left). Since the courses' openings in 1923 and 1924, they have been a popular destination for Los Angeles golfers.

GRIFFITH PARK TRAVEL TOWN, 1967. Around 1946, Los Angeles Department of Recreation and Parks employee Charley Atkins, a railroad enthusiast, created a steam locomotive ride with other railroad friends on the San Fernando Valley side of Griffith Park. They acquired two steam engines from the Los Angeles Harbor Department and contacted railroads to acquire more equipment. On December 14, 1952, Griffith Park Travel Town was dedicated. By 1965, Griffith Park Travel Town's exhibits were regrouped, and the park was improved and rededicated.

GRIFFITH PARK MINIATURE TRAIN, 1957. Miniature train rides featured a train built by the All-American Streamliner Company of Los Angeles. The trains are one-fourth and one-third scale models of actual locomotives and passenger cars. The miniature trains adjacent to the Griffith Park Pony Rides have been operating continuously since 1948, except for a few years in the 1950s. The attraction reopened with a new train station and visitor center in 1957.

BEVERLY PARK AMUSEMENTS, 1946. For 28 years, the "kiddie" amusement park on the southwest corner of Beverly and La Cienega Boulevards was operated by entrepreneur Dave Bradley. The park featured a mini roller coaster, Ferris wheel, and carousels in two sizes. Bradley and partner Don Kaye leased property in 1945 from Beverly Oil Company. A traveling carnival company had left rides on the site, which the partners took over. In 1946, Beverly Park Children's Amusement Center opened. Bradley's friend, Walt Disney, brought his kids to the park as he contemplated some day opening a similar attraction.

BEVERLY PONYLAND, 1947. Universal-International Pictures film star Dan Duryea visits Beverly Ponyland with his two sons, Peter and Richard, on a publicity tour. Ponyland was opened in the early 1940s by Pat Murphy, who rented Welsh ponies for children's amusement. Located on the southeast corner of Beverly and San Vicente Boulevards, the pony rides attracted families in the area that already were attending the adjacent Beverly Park Amusements. Ponyland ceased operations after 40 years and was replaced by the Beverly Center.

Three

HOTELS AND MOTELS

Hollywood tourist destinations since the 19th century included the Paul DeLongpre Mansion and the Bernheimer "Yamashiro" Estate, high in the hills above the residential community. When the entertainment industry began to locate in Hollywood, tourists would come to get a glimpse of movie stars or to take studio tours, which had been instituted at Universal Studios as early as 1915. At the beginning of the 20th century, only one large hotel was located in town, with small bed-and-breakfasts nearby. The Hollywood Hotel was established at Highland Avenue and Hollywood Boulevard in 1903. More and larger hotels were built to handle the growing population and visitors.

The important hotels built in the 1920s included the Hollywood Knickerbocker (1925), Hollywood Plaza (1925), and Hollywood Roosevelt (1927). Decades passed before another major hotel was built as these historic accommodations fostered a Hollywood celebrity culture that continues to this day. The Hollywood Hotel was demolished to make way for development in the 1950s, and the Hollywood Plaza and the Hollywood Knickerbocker became apartment-hotels. The Hollywood Roosevelt Hotel has maintained its historic landmark presence as a tourist hotel over the decades.

Smaller but important hotels built in the 1920s and 1930s included the Christie, Mark Twain, Gilbert, and Harvey Hotels, all catering to entertainment industry workers. The 1940s and 1950s brought a boom in motels. Some were carved out of surviving farmhouses and others were designed using streamline moderne architectural details or old California Spanish Colonial style. The major hotels in the 1950s renovated their buildings by adding swimming pools and other amenities as a result of the competition between them and the smaller hotels.

The Holiday Inn opened in the heart of Hollywood in 1968. At this time, the old hotels had lost their traditional clientele due to better and more luxurious hotels in Beverly Hills and Los Angeles. They fell into disrepair and turned into mixed-use hotel apartments. Tourists were still coming to Hollywood, but at the beginning of the 1970s were finding the area run-down and not tourist-friendly. By 1969, most of the tourists visiting Hollywood were staying at either the Hollywood Holiday Inn or the newly opened Sheraton Universal Hotel at Universal City.

HOLLYWOOD HOTEL, 1956. On April 30, 1956, the Old-Timers Club of Hollywood held a final dinner in the hotel's dining room. C. E. Toberman, the pioneer developer who originally purchased the hotel property, attended. On May 4, the wreckers began dismantling the old building, which had been a Hollywood landmark since its first wing was built in 1903.

THE HOLLYWOOD HOTEL LOBBY, 1956. The last guest checks out of the famed hotel in July 1956 while it was being dismantled. A major landmark throughout the early pioneering days of Hollywood, it survived for more than 50 years on the northwest corner of Hollywood Boulevard and Highland Avenue. Many a celebrity either stayed at the hotel or was a Grand Ballroom party guest, including Rudolph Valentino, Charles Chaplin, Douglas Fairbanks, Mary Pickford, and Norma Talmadge.

HOLLYWOOD HOTEL DEMOLITION, 1956. By September, much of the old hotel was gone and replaced by a high-rise office tower built by C. E. Toberman. The Hollywood Florist, one of the oldest hotel tenants, relocated nearby, and its sign was one of the last vestiges of the vanishing hotel. The tower was supposed to combine a hotel and shopping center, but after its February 23, 1959, opening, the project was never realized except for an underground parking structure.

HOLLYWOOD PLAZA HOTEL, 1944.
Located at 1637 North Vine Street, one building south of Hollywood Boulevard, the Plaza opened in 1925. Hollywood real estate pioneer Jacob Stern built it on his residential estate, and the original palm trees he planted at the beginning of the 20th century can be seen at the hotel's rear. The front was known as "the Doorway of Hospitality."

PLAZA HOTEL, 1947. Many radio, television, and music stars stayed at the Plaza to be close to the nearby studios. The street-level ballroom later became the famous It Café of Clara Bow. When Bette Davis came to Hollywood for the first time, she and her mother stayed at the Plaza in 1930. Comedian George Burns had an office on top of the hotel in the late 1930s. The Plaza, located just south of Hollywood Boulevard and Vine Street, became an important tourist hotel in the 1940s and 1950s.

PLAZA HOTEL LOBBY, 1941. This is the last photograph of the lobby area of the Plaza Hotel before World War II, showing the original Italian-coffered ceiling, bronze chandeliers, and some original furnishings. After the war, the small but intimate lobby was modernized by removing the Old World–style architectural details and furnishings that were dominant during the 1920s.

HOLLYWOOD KNICKERBOCKER HOTEL, 1950. Located at 1714 North Ivar Avenue, half a block north of Hollywood Boulevard, the Hollywood Knickerbocker Hotel was the first luxury hotel to open in Hollywood, in 1925, since the Hollywood Hotel in 1903. Designed in Spanish Colonial elegance, the hotel had 500 rooms and 200 suites. After the 1929 Wall Street crash, the hotel was reinvented as an "apartment hotel." Celebrities who frequented the hotel included Rudolph Valentino, Cecil B. DeMille, Blanche Sweet, and Ruth Roland.

KNICKERBOCKER HOTEL LOBBY, 1940. Old World charm was the dominant style of the 1920s when the hotel opened. Italian, Spanish, and French styles converged into an intimate lobby that was the most elegant in Hollywood. This is the lobby where the great cinema director D. W. Griffith collapsed and died in July 1948. During the 1940s, the hotel was known as "the Hotel of the Stars" and "Home of the Famous."

TERRACE ROOM, 1940. A popular restaurant in Hollywood was the Knickerbocker's Terrace Room, where many celebrities dined. Advertisements placed it in the "Heart of Hollywood" and "A Whisper off Hollywood Boulevard where Famous Stars of the Entertainment World Meet." Some of them included Mae West, Hedda Hopper, John Boles, Edward Arnold, Robert Taylor, Barbara Stanwyck, Tyrone Power, Frank Sinatra, and Elvis Presley, who stayed in room 1016 while making *Love Me Tender* in 1956.

HOLLYWOOD ROOSEVELT HOTEL, 1952. Opened in 1927 at 7006 Hollywood Boulevard, the Roosevelt Hotel was and still is a major landmark. With 400 rooms in 12 stories, the hotel was originally the home of the Academy Awards and has hosted countless industry functions. The original Spanish Colonial Revival architecture and details were covered during the 1940s and 1950s but were restored in the 1980s.

ROOSEVELT HOTEL'S RESORT WING, 1950. Opened on April 1, 1950, the Resort Wing was designed by architect Frank W. Green and contained 60 guest rooms with individual patio-sun decks surrounding a 30-by-75-foot tile swimming pool. The compound included a pool bar, snack bar, and tropical gardens, bringing back the Hollywood Roosevelt as a major tourist destination.

RESORT WING, 1951. When the Roosevelt Hotel's swimming pool opened in April 1950, the management at Hull Hotels publicized it; it was the hotel's first pool. It lured industry publicists to show off new talent by using the pool area as a background for photography shoots. Marilyn Monroe was photographed at the pool, and it was reported that she stayed in room 1200 for a time in the mid-1950s.

ROOSEVELT HOTEL BROCHURE, 1961. The Resort Wing is featured in this Hull Hotels brochure, which stated, "A luxurious subtropical garden retreat in the heart of glamorous Hollywood with a spacious sun-lazing area surrounding an Olympic-sized swimming pool and a poolside bar and al fresco dining." The brochure goes on to say that the hotel is the "home of the world famous Cinegrill, Blossom Room, and Garden Room."

ROOSEVELT HOTEL LOBBY, 1986. The newly restored lobby was brought back to nearly its original decor of 1927. The Larel Hotels Inc., opened the hotel in January 1986 with 304 restored and enlarged rooms and 80 cabana rooms in the Resort Wing. The lobby's Spanish Revival decor included an original custom-made brass chandelier that was found in the basement and restored to a ceiling that was also refurbished—by the same family that painted it originally in 1927.

HOLLYWOOD INN, 1958. Located at 6724 Hollywood Boulevard, at McCadden Place, this hotel was originally opened in 1923 as the Christie Hotel for entertainment business clientele. By 1945, the hotel changed hands, was renamed the Hollywood Drake Hotel, and included two well-known restaurant-bars, the Hunt Room and the London Grill. The hotel changed ownership again and reopened in January 1958 as the Hollywood Inn.

HOTEL MARK TWAIN, 1948. Located at 1622 North Wilcox Avenue between Hollywood Boulevard and Selma Avenue, these accommodations originally opened in 1924. By 1927, the hotel had changed hands twice. Edwin R. Ardis, a real estate agent, purchased it sometime around 1926 and sold it to Craig D. Pierce in 1927. By 1931, the hotel was sold again to William F. Pierce, formerly of Seattle.

GILBERT HOTEL, 1966. One of the small hotels just off Hollywood Boulevard, the Gilbert Hotel is located at 1150 North Wilcox Avenue, near Hotel Mark Twain. The Gilbert Hotel was advertised as the "Drive In" hotel with 70 rooms, all with bathrooms, and "Your Home Away From Home." Opened in 1926 in a three-story brick and concrete building, the hotel advertised its 80-space garage included in the room rent. A patio garden with an electric fountain were in the front of the hotel.

HOTEL HARVEY, 1965. This neighborhood hotel is located at 5640 Santa Monica Boulevard. The hotel had 200 rooms and baths, catered to industry professionals, and advertised a location in the "center of Hollywood Studio activity."

HOLIDAY INN HOLLYWOOD, 1968. Seen under construction, the Holiday Inn was the largest hotel built in Hollywood at the time, catering to the 1960s tourism boom. The *Los Angeles Times* announced, "Major Hollywood Hotel to be Built Since '27," at 1747 North Highland Avenue. It was the first "major" hotel since the Hollywood Roosevelt Hotel in 1927. In 1970, the Holiday Inn opened Oscar's Restaurant/Nightclub atop the building, with a 360-degree view of Hollywood.

HYATT ON SUNSET BOULEVARD, 1979. Originally opened as Gene Autry's Hotel Continental in 1963, this 13-story, 300-room hotel is located at 8401 Sunset Boulevard, on the Sunset Strip. The Hotel Continental was developed by Saul Pick, who took over the old Columbia Studios and converted it to a rental lot. The hotel site was 65,000-square feet at Sunset Boulevard and Kings Road. The hotel, the first built on the Strip in many years, was designed by Martin Stern Jr.

SHERATON UNIVERSAL HOTEL, 1969. Known as the "Hotel of the Stars," the Sheraton Universal Hotel was built by the Music Corporation of America (MCA) under a long-term lease by the Sheraton Corporation of America. On a hill overlooking the Cahuenga Pass, the 12-story hotel was the first phase of a major development of Universal land surrounding the studio that later became Universal CityWalk. Architect William B. Tabler designed the 500-room hotel, which opened on February 15, 1969.

SUNSET ORANGE MOTEL, 1959. Across the street from Hollywood High School at 1501 North Orange Drive, on the northwest corner of Sunset Boulevard, this motel opened in the mid-1950s and was operated by a Las Vegas concern. A socioeconomic decline in the 1970s turned the area into a hangout for prostitutes and drug deals. By the 1980s, the area was cleaned up.

HALLMARK MOTEL, 1966. One of the many Hollywood motels lining Sunset Boulevard, the Hallmark, with its Hallmark House restaurant, swimming pool, and underground parking at 7023 Sunset Boulevard, serviced the large tourist trade. The name was changed to the Days Inn Hollywood in the 1990s.

RIVIERA MOTEL, 1966. Located on the northwest corner of Sunset Boulevard and McCadden Place, this 1950s-style motel was one of many on Sunset Boulevard. One block from Hollywood High School, the Riviera Motel had a small swimming pool. By the 1990s, the motel was demolished.

HOLLYWOOD VINE MOTEL, 1966. Located at 1133 North Vine Street, this motel was designed in a U-shaped form and included a swimming pool and kitchenettes. Centrally located in Hollywood just north of Santa Monica Boulevard, the Hollywood Vine Motel was a member of the Friendship Inns of America and catered to the tourist trade and industry professionals. Around 2002, the motel became the Vagabond Inn of Hollywood.

YUCCA MOTEL, 1951. Built in the late 1940s, the Yucca Motel was located in the center of Hollywood at 1822 North Cahuenga Boulevard and was advertised as the "newest and finest in Hollywood." By the 1990s, the motel changed names to the Best Inn and was remodeled.

Four

RESIDENCES

Developed out of farms and ranches in the 19th century, Hollywood became a city in its own right in 1903. After annexation to Los Angeles in 1910, businesses began to take over the residential main streets, such as Prospect Avenue, which was later renamed Hollywood Boulevard, pushing the larger residences into the overlooking hills. The residential developments of Whitley Heights, Hollywoodland, Outpost Estates, and others were in a state of suspension by 1940 due to the economic downturn of the Great Depression of the 1930s. New housing in the early 1940s was suspended again during World War II.

Among the more historic residential landmarks that still existed in the 1940s was Yamashiro, formerly known as the Bernheimer estate. It was built in 1911 on a hill overlooking Hollywood. The Rollin B. Lane mansion was built just below it. In 1948, the entire hill was purchased by the Glover family, who restored and eventually leased the existing Bernheimer buildings for a restaurant named the Yamashiro and the Lane mansion as the Magic Castle Club for magicians.

The Hollywoodland Development, touted as the "Beverly Hills" of Hollywood, was begun in 1923 and resulted in many houses being built in the 1920s. But the boom was suspended during the Depression and war. One of the most important landmarks in Hollywoodland is Castillo Del Lago, built in 1926 and owned by pop singer Madonna in more recent times. Other Hollywood mansions still existing by 1940 in Hollywood included the Janes sister's house at Hollywood Boulevard and Whitley Avenue. Somehow the Janes house still exists as a restaurant and has survived for over 100 years on Hollywood Boulevard. Most of the early Hollywood mansions have disappeared over time, but a majority in the hills have survived and are now in demand due to their craftsmanship and beauty.

OLIVE HILL, EAST HOLLYWOOD, 1947. This view of Olive Hill at the corner of Sunset Boulevard and Vermont Avenue (far right) shows that a large undeveloped parcel still existed in Hollywood as late as 1950. Acquired in 1920 by Aline Barnsdall for her estate, Olive Hill became a Frank Lloyd Wright project as the architect created a unique house for her. Aline Barnsdall eventually donated the entire property to the City of Los Angeles. Today Barnsdall Park contains Hollyhock House, Hollyhock House Gallery, Los Angeles Municipal Art Gallery, Barnsdall Art Center, and Barnsdall Park Theatre.

YAMASHIRO, 1949. Construction of the house began in 1911 by the Bernheimer brothers, who imported Oriental art. *Yamashiro* means "mountain palace" in Japanese, and its namesake became an enduring landmark. Japanese craftsmen were brought in to recreate a palace in the Yamashiro Mountains near Kyoto, Japan. By 1914, the estate with Japanese gardens was completed. By the 1920s, it was taken over by the 400 Club, a film industry fund-raising group. In 1948, Thomas O. Glover purchased the estate, and his son Tom Y. Glover opened Yamashiro Restaurant in 1959.

CASTILLO DEL LAGO, 1960. Construction was completed in June 1926 on this landmark, which could be seen for miles. Nestled above Hollywoodland, the Tower Hill castle was designed by John DeLario for oilman Patrick M. Longan. Located at 6342 Mulholland Highway, the Spanish-Mediterranean castle overlooks Lake Hollywood. It was rumored that gangster Bugsy Siegel leased Tower Hill for a speakeasy around 1938. In 1963, 20th Century Fox used the estate as a location for *House of the Damned*. Thirty years later, pop singer Madonna bought Tower Hill and painted it terra-cotta with light yellow stripes.

CASTLE ARGYLE, 1944. A permit was issued to build a first-class, high-rise apartment house to Dr. A. G. Castles in April 1928. Dr. Castles had changed his name from Schloesser during World War I and built Castle Sans Souci near the corner of Franklin and Argyle Avenues. The new apartment house, located at 1919 North Argyle Avenue, was not completed before Dr. Castles went bankrupt due to the stock market crash. The bank finished the building and later sold it to former film producer Phil Goldstone.

VILLA CARLOTTA, 1940. The Ince Investment Company built the Villa Carlotta Apartments at Tamarind and Franklin Avenues in 1926. Eleanor Ince, the widow of pioneering producer Thomas H. Ince, owned the building and also constructed and owned the Chateau Elysee, across the street. The four-story, Spanish- and Italian-designed Carlotta at 5959 Franklin Avenue had 51 apartments. The apartments were built as soundproof rooms, and many were later rented by singers. In 1953, Glen Wallich, a founder of Capitol Records, bought the apartments. Stars who lived there included Kim Novak.

FONTENOY, 1950. An advertisement on April 9, 1929, claimed that a new apartment house was to be constructed in French Normandy style by Dr. S. M. Wells at 1811 North Whitley Avenue. The house was named the Fontenoy and would have 48 corner apartments with a subterranean garage. The new apartment house opened on April 10, 1929, and was touted as "the first of its kind on the Pacific Coast." It was a Class-A, steel-concrete building designed by architect Leland A. Bryant.

GARDEN COURT. One of Hollywood's important landmarks for over 60 years, the Garden Court opened formally in February 1917. The Italian Renaissance–style building was to be a "showplace of Hollywood." Located at 7021 Hollywood Boulevard, the apartment house became a social center in Hollywood for 30 years and became Los Angeles Cultural Landmark No. 243 on April 28, 1981. It was demolished in 1984.

HOTEL WILCOX, 1948. This five-story structure was built by architect and builder Thomas B. Morrison for Dr. A. E. Shaw at 6504 Selma Avenue in 1926. The Hotel Wilcox catered to industry workers arriving in Hollywood. Located "in the heart of Hollywood," it had 80 rooms with baths and radios in every room. By 1951, there were seven stores on the ground floor with a corner drugstore.

FRENCH VILLAGE, 1939. Built at 2306–2320 North Highland Avenue, this French-themed apartment house was advertised thusly in 1928: "These apartments were built with the idea of furnishing attractive homes and gardens for people who derive pleasure from living in artistic surroundings in the center of Hollywood." Located at Highland Avenue and Cahuenga Boulevard, the French Village became a Cahuenga Pass landmark until it was removed for the Hollywood Freeway in 1952.

ROMAN GARDENS, 1940. Built in 1926 at 2000 North Highland Avenue in the Cahuenga Pass south of Milner Avenue, the Italian, Spanish, and Moorish-style building was designed by Walter S. Davis. The Roman Gardens, declared Los Angeles Landmark No. 397 on November 23, 1988, still stands.

VOLTAIRE, 1947. Located in West Hollywood at 1424–1428 North Crescent Heights just south of Sunset Boulevard, the Voltaire was one of the most luxurious apartment houses built at the beginning of the Depression. Designed by architect Leland Bryant, the seven-story structure of French Regency style was the largest apartment building in West Hollywood.

HIGHLAND TOWERS, 1948. The Cahuenga Pass was once a residential neighborhood with a two-lane road connecting Hollywood to the San Fernando Valley. The intersection of Franklin and Highland Avenues was a center of neighborhood activity with Whitley Heights to the east of Highland behind the building. The Highland Towers was built at 1922 North Highland Avenue. Tenants included May Robson and Thelma Todd with her mother.

EL ROYALE, 1944. Opened in July 1929 at 450 North Rossmore Avenue in South Hollywood, architect William Douglas Lee's El Royale was designed in the Spanish-French Renaissance style. The 12-story building overlooks the Wilshire Country Club. In advertisements it was touted as, "An Address of Distinction." Other advertisements listed such amenities as garages, roof gardens, children's playground, park, tennis courts, and putting green. Rents ranged from $170 to $900. Celebrities who once lived there included Harry Langdon, Helen Morgan, and George Raft.

LIDO, 1944. Originally built in 1929 at 6500 Yucca Street, the five-story, 138-unit Lido has catered to movie professionals. The Lido's unusual curved exterior with Spanish Colonial style was designed by architect F. A. Brown. Warner Brothers star Frank McHugh lived there in the 1930s. The building was remodeled into an apartment-hotel in 1955 and included two swimming pools. Photographs on the Eagles' album, *Hotel California*, were taken at the Lido in the 1970s.

Five

FILM STUDIOS

Film studios literally replaced the small residential suburb of Hollywood with one of the most important new industries in history. The 1920s brought a boom in studio construction and with the coming of sound films in 1927, this boom continued, adding sound stages and other facilities to existing studio lots all over Los Angeles. By the 1930s, the silent-era studios were either incorporated into more modern studio lots or had disappeared. Hollywood was where many of the existing studios survive as working historic landmarks.

The sound era began unprecedented construction programs expanding and modernizing facilities. The era of "farmhouse" studios was over. Most of the studios today that still exist have the same infrastructure built in the 1930s and 1940s and only recently have been modernized and restored. Some studios were totally remodeled with most of their original buildings replaced. Universal Studios has been located at its present site since 1912 and has undergone several major renovation and modernization programs since MCA took over in 1960, completing them in 1964. In the mid-1980s, Universal Studios demolished most of its back lot.

Other major studio historic landmarks in Hollywood that make up a major portion of tourist destinations in Hollywood today include the Desilu Gower Studio, which was merged with Paramount in 1967 (originally the RKO Studios from 1928 to 1957); the Monogram Pictures Studios in East Hollywood that later became KCET-TV Public Broadcasting Studios; and Raleigh Studios, which is one of the oldest but still active rental studios in Hollywood (since 1915). Raleigh originally was the Clune Film Producing Studios, then the Douglas Fairbanks Studio, Tec Art, Prudential, Enterprise, California, and finally Producers Studio (1961).

LASKY-DEMILLE BARN, 1956. On December 27, 1956, the famed Lasky-DeMille Barn, the birthplace of what is known today as Paramount Studios, was dedicated California State Landmark No. 554 as "Hollywood's First Major Film Company Studio" by the California State Parks Commission and the Landmarks Committee of Los Angeles County. The dedication ceremony took place adjacent to the Paramount Studio's Western town set with Paramount founders Jesse Lasky, Sam Goldwyn, Cecil B. DeMille, and Adolph Zukor attending. The barn was the first studio used by the Lasky Feature Play Company to produce Hollywood's first feature-length motion picture, *The Squaw Man,* in late 1913. Today the old barn is now the Hollywood Heritage Museum.

LASKY-DEMILLE BARN, 1992. The Lasky Feature Play Company Studio was once located on the southeast corner of Selma Avenue and Vine Street. The barn was moved to Paramount Studios on Marathon Street in 1926 when the studio relocated there. The barn was moved again to a parking lot on Vine Street on October 25, 1979. Hollywood Heritage Inc., acquired the barn from the Hollywood Chamber of Commerce and moved it again to its present site on February 15, 1983, and opened as the Hollywood Studio Museum. Today the old former studio of Cecil B. DeMille was renamed the Hollywood Heritage Museum and contains historic artifacts from motion picture studios.

SAMUEL GOLDWYN STUDIOS, 1939. This studio lot dates to 1919 when it was the Jesse D. Hampton Studios. By 1922, Douglas Fairbanks and Mary Pickford acquired the lot and renamed it the Pickford-Fairbanks Studios at 7200 Santa Monica Boulevard. The studio became United Artists in 1927. By 1937, Samuel Goldwyn acquired a majority of the United Artists stock. In 1938, Goldwyn changed the name to Samuel Goldwyn Studios with the gate now at 1041 North Formosa Avenue. In 1980, Warner Brothers Studios acquired it and renamed it Warner Hollywood Studios. In 1999, the studio was renamed The Lot.

COLUMBIA STUDIOS, 1940. Originally established on Gower Street in 1924, this studio gradually expanded to neighboring properties. Some of the classic films made on this lot from 1940 include *He Stayed For Breakfast* (1940) starring Loretta Young (see billboard on the side of the stage), *Cover Girl* (1944) with Rita Hayworth, *From Here To Eternity* (1953) with Frank Sinatra and Montgomery Clift, *On the Waterfront (1954)* with Marlon Brando, and *The Caine Mutiny* (1954) with Humphrey Bogart.

SUNSET GOWER INDEPENDENT STUDIOS, 2003. Columbia Studios moved from their studio lot of 48 years to Burbank in conjunction with Warner Brothers, forming the Burbank Studios in 1972. For years, the old Columbia lot was abandoned except for Filmex (Film Exposition of Los Angeles) offices on Beachwood Drive. In 1977, television producer Nick Vanoff along with his partners purchased the studio and changed the name to the Sunset Gower Independent Studios.

DESILU GOWER STUDIOS, 1958. RKO Studios at 780 North Gower Street was put up for sale in 1957. The strange irony in its purchase was that it was by a former RKO starlet, Lucille Ball. With her husband, Desi Arnaz, Lucy made RKO's Gower Street property part of their Desilu empire. Ball and Arnaz took possession of the lot in 1958. The deal included the RKO-Pathe Studios in Culver City, which added stage and back lot facilities to their already existing studio on Cahuenga Boulevard.

DESILU CAHUENGA STUDIOS, 1956. The former Motion Picture Center Studios was acquired by Desilu in late 1953 as a permanent home for the *I Love Lucy* show. This view is the east side of the studio located at 811 Lillian Way, where studio audiences would line up waiting to get into *The Dick Van Dyke Show, Danny Thomas Show, Our Miss Brooks,* and *The Jack Benny Show.*

MONOGRAM PICTURES STUDIOS, 1941. Located at 4376 Sunset Drive (now KCET Studios), the Monogram Pictures Studios lot dates to 1912 when it was known as the Lubin Film Company, then Essanay (1913), Kalem (1915), Charles Ray (1920), International (1920s–1930s), Monogram (1941), and KCET-TV (1971). Monogram Pictures Studios was known for B pictures featuring the Eastside Kids, Cisco Kid, and Charlie Chan.

CHAPLIN/SKELTON STUDIOS, 1962. After Charles Chaplin sold his studio in 1952, it passed through different companies, such as Kling Television Studios (1953–1958), American International Pictures (1958–1960), Red Skelton Studios (1960–1962), CBS Television Network (1962–1966), A&M Records (1966–1989), PolyGram Studio (1989–1998), Seagram/Universal Music Group (1998–1999), and Jim Henson Company Lot (1999–present). Shows filmed on the lot include *Perry Mason* (1957–1966), *Superman* (1952–1957), and *The Red Skelton Show* (1952–1970).

RALEIGH STUDIOS, 1982. Formerly the Producers Studio (1961–1979), this studio at 650 North Bronson Avenue is one of Hollywood's longest continuously operating studios (since 1915). The first *Superman* pilot for television and *Gunsmoke* were shot here, as well as films featuring stars whose careers spanned the decades, such as Charles Chaplin, Douglas Fairbanks, Mary Pickford, Ingrid Bergman, and Frank Sinatra. Recently Raleigh hosted such shows as *Ugly Betty* and *The Closer*.

CALIFORNIA STUDIOS, 1951. Originally opened in 1915 as the Famous Players Film Company and taken over by theater owner William H. Clune in the same year, the studio was leased to many companies over its long history. The Western town on the back lot was used by William Boyd for the *Hopalong Cassidy* series distributed by Paramount in the 1930s. Major companies on the lot included Douglas Fairbanks, Tec Art, Prudential, Harry Sherman, Enterprise, California, Producers, and Raleigh in 1979. Shows and pilots shot there included *Death Valley Days*, *Have Gun Will Travel*, and *Space Patrol*.

PARAMOUNT STUDIOS, 1947. Located on Marathon Street just east of Gower Street, the studio had moved there between 1926 and 1927 from their original site at Sunset Boulevard and Vine Street in Hollywood. The lot during the 1940s and 1950s was very busy with the making of such classic films as *The Black Cat* (1941) with Alan Ladd, *Double Indemnity* (1944) with Barbara Stanwyck, *The Blue Dahlia* (1946) with Alan Ladd, *Sunset Boulevard* (1949) with Gloria Swanson and William Holden, *Shane* (1953) with Alan Ladd, and *The Ten Commandments* (1956) starring Charlton Heston.

63

WARNER EAST HOLLYWOOD STUDIO ANNEX, 1941. In 1925, Warner Brothers bought the old Vitagraph Company's assets and used the studio as a back lot. Films and shows produced there include *The Jazz Singer* (1927), *Noah's Ark* (1928), *Captain Blood* (1935), and *The Sea Hawk* (1940). In 1948, the studio was sold to ABC-TV, which produced *The Lawrence Welk Show* (1955–1971), *American Bandstand* (1957–1987), *Let's Make a Deal* (1968–1976), and recently *The Shield* (2006) and *Grey's Anatomy* (2005). In 1996, ABC and Disney merged, and, by 2002, the studio's name became Prospect Studios.

GENERAL SERVICE STUDIOS, 1945. Currently known as Hollywood Center Studios at 1040 North Las Palmas Avenue, this facility opened in 1919 as the Hollywood Studios. It was renamed the Hollywood-Metropolitan Studios in 1927 and General Service Studios during the 1930s. In 1980, Francis Ford Coppola took over the lot and renamed it Zoetrope. Shows made on the lot include *The Burns and Allen Show* (1950), *I Love Lucy* (1951), *The Bob Cummings Show* (1952), *Adventures of Ozzie and Harriett* (1952), *Mr. Ed* (1961), and *The Beverly Hillbillies* (1962).

KCET-TV Studios, 2005. Los Angeles Public Broadcasting station KCET moved to East Hollywood in 1971. The studio at 4401 Sunset Boulevard was designated as Historic Cultural Monument No. 198 because it had been a film studio since 1912. National PBS series produced at the studio include *Hollywood Television Theater, Visions, Cosmos,* and *Life and Times.* KCET offered tours that included the 1933 screening room, the Little Theater, with its white columns, beamed ceiling, and brick walls.

Tribune Studios, 2004. Originally built by Warner Brothers in 1920 at 5858 Sunset Boulevard, this studio was the Warner Brother's base until the company moved to a larger studio in Burbank in 1928. The Sunset studio became an annex for shorts, films that are around one to two reels as opposed to the feature film that is at least five reels in length. In 1942, the lot was acquired by Paramount for the television unit KTLA. The main stage behind the administration building was converted into the Hollywood Bowling Lanes in the 1940s. In 1964, Gene Autry purchased KTLA and radio station KMPC, which were housed there. The Tribune Studios hosted such shows as *Judge Judy* and *Hannah Montana.*

UNIVERSAL PICTURES COMPANY, INC., 1940. Universal Studios was established in the township of Lankershim/North Hollywood in 1912. Some of the Universal Studios films and stars of the 1940s and 1950s include Deanna Durbin; Abbott and Costello; the *Arabian Nights* romances of Jon Hall and Maria Montez; the Basil Rathbone *Sherlock Holmes* series; and 1950s pictures starring James Stewart, Tony Curtis, and Rock Hudson.

MCA/UNIVERSAL, 1964. By 1964, much of the old Universal Studios lot was demolished by new owners MCA in a modernization effort. When Universal City Plaza Phase 1 was completed, a new black-glass building dominated the studio. Production added a new breed of producers, directors, and actors in the 1960s who were working more in television than in films. Alfred Hitchcock was brought to the lot with his television series *Alfred Hitchcock Presents* and his famous film *Psycho* (1960).

Six

BUSINESS COMMUNITY

Businesses of all types have flourished in Hollywood since its namesake boulevard became a shopping street in the 1920s. Some of Hollywood's more important business buildings were reused over the years by different retailers and services. A great example of this was the Hollywood Broadway Building at Hollywood Boulevard and Vine Street, since 1931. It closed in the 1980s after 50 years of service to the Hollywood community.

Only recently have restoration efforts by new businesses been undertaken to preserve historic and architectural beauty. The Technicolor building on Cahuenga was a major Hollywood landmark from the 1940s through the 1960s until it moved to Universal City. Today the UCLA Film and Television Archive is housed there. Near Western Avenue, the Sears and Roebuck Company building, constructed in the 1920s, serviced the neighborhood until 2008. On Hollywood Boulevard, the Barker Brothers Company furnished celebrity homes since the 1920s. Two newsstands have lasted for more than 60 years: Universal News Agency on Las Palmas Avenue (closed in 2008) and the World Book and News on Cahuenga Boulevard near Hollywood Boulevard.

Many of the high-rise buildings on Hollywood Boulevard were built in the 1930s. The beautiful Equitable Building traditionally housed entertainment companies along with some agencies representing talent into the 1960s. The California Bank Building at Selma Avenue and Vine Street, built in the late 1940s, began a trend of cheaper, one-story buildings to house banks and stores. On September 12, 1951, a plaque was placed on the south wall of the bank to commemorate the "first feature film made in Hollywood" by the Lasky Feature Play Company (across the street on the southeast corner). Former Lasky company celebrities in attendance included Jesse Lasky, Cecil B. DeMille, and Samuel Goldwyn.

Cultural or architectural landmarks include the 1922-vintage Lyon Van and Storage Building and the Hollywood Greyhound Bus station. Hollywood movie palaces were integrated with stores facing Hollywood Boulevard. The Warner Theater building had several stores in it, including Stromberg Jewelers with their signature sidewalk clock, a landmark on the boulevard for over 20 years.

HOLLYWOOD AND CAHUENGA BOULEVARDS, 1943. The southeast corner of Hollywood and Cahuenga Boulevards was where the original old Hollywood Civic Center was located. The old city hall was known as Wilcox Hall. In 1933, the site was redeveloped with the entire block demolished and replaced with a streamline moderne–style structure named the Julian Medical Building. The Beveridge family (Daeida Wilcox Beveridge), who built Wilcox Hall, financed the development.

TECHNICOLOR LABORATORY, 1940. Technicolor Corporation expanded their facilities and built a major laboratory on Cahuenga Boulevard at Romaine Street. The two-story reinforced concrete structure built by the Austin Company with art deco styling opened on February 1, 1939.

SEARS, 1930. In May 1928, the Sears Roebuck and Company of Chicago opened several stores in Los Angeles, the third of which was in Hollywood. On May 27, preliminary construction of this new store was executed by Scofield-Twaltz Company, contractors on Santa Monica Boulevard at St. Andrews Place. A formal grand opening was held on October 4, 1928, for the three-story building, which had a large tower designed in Spanish Colonial Revival style.

EL CAPITAN/BARKER BROTHERS, 1947. Hollywood developer C. E. Toberman built the El Capitan Building at 6838–6840 Hollywood Boulevard in 1926. The theater opened as a legitimate stage, with the Barker Brothers Furniture Company taking over the commercial portion. After a premiere opening, Hollywood residents would step next door to buy furniture and decorations. Director Cecil B. DeMille bought authentic American Indian rugs for his ranch house. Barker Brothers remained for 42 years, until 1968.

UNIVERSAL NEWS AGENCY, 1947. A commercial structure was built in 1936 on the southwest corner of Hollywood Boulevard and Las Palmas, where the Universal News Agency stand opened at 1655 North Las Palmas (later changed to 1639 Las Palmas). The newsstand touted its importance with a sign that read, "The World's Largest Outdoor Newsstand—Open 24 hours every day." It closed in 2008.

EQUITABLE BUILDING, 1948. Constructed in two phases, this Hollywood landmark was built as the Bank of Hollywood in 1929 on the northeast corner of Hollywood Boulevard and Vine Street. By April 1930, the second tower was begun, and the dual-tower building opened in January 1931 as the Equitable Building. By August 1931, the California Bank moved into the ground floor. Later the Myron Selznick Agency, which represented such stars as Laurence Olivier, Vivien Leigh, and Henry Fonda, moved in.

THE OUTPOST BUILDING, 1949. Built in 1927 by Mr. and Mrs. B. C. Donnelly and their architect B. B. Horner, the two-unit building of Spanish Colonial architecture was an unusual addition to the boulevard at that time. The first floor contained studio shops with 19-foot ceilings and mezzanine balconies, modeled after shops in Madrid, Spain.

CALIFORNIA BANK, 1949. On September 7, 1947, construction began on a new bank and office structure on the northeast corner of Selma Avenue and Vine Street. The building was one and a half stories in height and faced with pink Utah sandstone, using a base trim of Carnelian granite. A year later, on September 17, 1948, the official opening of the California Bank Building was attended by Dorothy Lamour, the first official depositor.

THE BROADWAY, 1951. By 1940, the Broadway Hollywood hosted lectures by noted writers and newspaper columnists on current events. Lee Shippey, a *Los Angeles Times* writer, was a regular speaker in the Little Theater. *Vogue,* the fashion magazine still in publication, hosted "A Fashion Review." During World War II, columnist Hedda Hopper reported on events at the Broadway. On November 24, 1953, a plaque unveiling was held on the corner of Hollywood and Vine Street in conjunction with Hollywood's 50th anniversary.

HOLLYWOOD SAVINGS AND LOAN, 1954. Located at 7051 Hollywood Boulevard, the Hollywood Savings building is of Greek and Mediterranean design and has been a landmark for 70-plus years. The bank's association with Hollywood goes back to 1948 when it financed the construction of a new prefabricated model home in Bel Air in conjunction with RKO Pictures film *Mr. Blandings Builds His Dream House,* starring Cary Grant and Myrna Loy.

LYON VAN AND STORAGE, 1952. One of Hollywood's oldest storage buildings, the Lyon company is located at 6372 Santa Monica Boulevard on the southeastern corner of Cahuenga and Santa Monica Boulevards. Originally opened in 1922 as the Premier Fireproof Storage Company in a five-story building with a Florentine-styled clock tower on the corner, it was used predominately by the industry to store equipment and props.

HOLLYWOOD GREYHOUND BUS STATION, 1956. Built in the 1950s, the Hollywood station for Greyhound at 1409 North Vine Street was a major depot for people coming to Hollywood from around the world. This station had several locations before settling here. During World War II, this Greyhound Bus station was at capacity, bringing servicemen from around the world to Hollywood.

WARNER THEATER BUILDING, 1958. Opened in 1928 at Wilcox Avenue and Hollywood Boulevard, this theater, when this photograph was taken, was exhibiting the Cinerama presentation *Seven Wonders of the World* in its second year of release. The famous William Stromberg Jewelers opened at 6439 Hollywood Boulevard around 1947 and erected its signature neon clock sign on the sidewalk. That clock was replaced in the early 1980s, along with Freeman Shoes and Mitchell's Fine Men's Wear.

WALLICH'S MUSIC CITY, 1956. In 1940, brothers Glenn and Clyde Wallich moved their business into a new building at the northwest corner of Sunset Boulevard and Vine Street. Repairing radios and selling records, they expanded their store to include sheet music and musical instruments. Weekly customers included Frank Sinatra, Mary Pickford, and Fred Astaire. By the late 1940s, Music City was one of leading television stores. By the 1950s, it sold everything that had to do with music. The store became the first to utilize record browsing racks and demonstration rooms for record buying.

CAPITOL RECORDS TOWER, 1958.
By 1942, Glenn Wallich and
songwriters Buddy DeSylva and
Johnny Mercer formed Capitol
Records Company and established
their offices on the second floor of
the Music City building at Sunset
Boulevard and Vine Street. By
1954, the new company needed
larger quarters. For two years,
Hollywood residents watched as
the first circular office building
in the world was constructed.
Designed by Welton Becket
Company and opened in 1956, the
13-story structure at 1750 North
Vine Street contains three studios
constructed on layers of cork with
shock-mounted reverberation
chambers underneath. A roof
beacon signals, in Morse code,
"H-O-L-L-Y-W-O-O-D."

CAPITOL NEWS, 1948. On one of the
Capitol Records News brochures, The King
Cole Trio is featured with Nat King Cole
at the right. This issue was published in
July 1948. Articles included are "Ciro's
Looms for King Cole Trio," "(Cocoanut)
Grove Wants (Freddie) Martin Back,"
"Frankie Laine Due This Month," and
"Top Singers Moving to West Coast."

HOLLYWOOD RANCH MARKET, 1961. Located at Vine Street and La Mirada Avenue adjacent to the Filmarte Theatre, the Ranch Market was a Hollywood landmark. When *The Steve Allen Show* was located at the Filmarte Theatre, Allen frequently referenced the market on the air. It was open 24 hours, and he performed some comedy stunts on La Mirada Avenue between the theater and the market. He also interviewed late-night shoppers in his "man on the street" segments.

SUNSET-VINE TOWER MODEL, 1963. Located on the southeast corner of Sunset Boulevard and Vine Street, the Sunset-Vine Tower opened in June 1963 and was 22 stories. Los Angeles Federal Savings, which occupied the ground floor, owned it. Architect John Rex of Honnold and Rex designed the building, which was constructed of Kaiser steel. It was one of the first of purely tower designs in the West. Al Gordon's Room at the Top opened in 1965 with a 360-degree view of the entire Los Angeles Basin.

Seven

RESTAURANTS AND NIGHTCLUBS

The celebrities, producers, moguls, writers, and all the workers at the various studios in Hollywood lived in the area and patronized the stores, offices, theaters, hotels, restaurants, and nightclubs. The premiere Hollywood restaurant icon that became world famous represented the Hollywood Brown Derby restaurants. The original "Hat" restaurant across from the Ambassador Hotel began the historic legacy that is still written about to this day. The Hollywood Brown Derby opened in 1929, attracting Hollywood stars, and became a gathering place for business and publicity.

The other enduring restaurants and nightclubs in Hollywood included Musso and Frank, which is still a great tourist attraction; Barney's Beanery in West Hollywood, a former simple roadhouse popular for 50 years; Whisky A Go Go on the Sunset Strip, which opened in 1966 and attracts visitors from around the world; and Miceli's Pizzeria in Hollywood, which opened its doors on Las Palmas in 1949 and continues to be a popular Hollywood restaurant.

Restaurants and nightclubs that helped make Hollywood famous and did not survive include the Hollywood Canteen (1942), where 600 stars entertained the troops during World War II; Florentine Gardens (1938), where floor show–style, pre–Las Vegas entertainment was popular; Schwab's Pharmacy at the beginning of the Sunset Strip, where director Billy Wilder shot scenes for *Sunset Boulevard*; the Players Club (1940), opened by director Preston Sturges, which housed a little theater to showcase plays featuring Hollywood stars; Nickodell (1954) with two branches; Mocambo (1941), the Sunset Strip venue with live parrots; and Ciro's (1940), the most popular restaurant-club on the Strip with a stellar clientele.

Near the Mocambo was the Trocadero Café (1934), one of the Strip's early nightclubs, which was later eclipsed in popularity by the Mocambo and Ciro's. In central Hollywood, Sardi's (1932) boasted architectural and interior design by Rudolph Schindler, and the Villa Capri (1939) on McCadden Place was one of the few restaurants that had Frank Sinatra as one of the investors. Nearby was Don the Beachcomber (1937), Hollywood's most exotic restaurant.

HOLLYWOOD BROWN DERBY, 1950. By 1940, the Derby was still one of the most important landmarks in Hollywood, where stars and executives dined regularly. The Derby in Hollywood was one of four and the second to be built. The Hollywood Brown Derby was remodeled for a new generation in the 1960s, closed in 1985, burned in 1988, and demolished in 1994.

HOLLYWOOD BROWN DERBY, 1949. One of the great restaurants in Hollywood, the Hollywood Brown Derby on Vine Street was where one could see and be seen with stars at any given time. In this photograph are Jimmy Durante, Peter Lorre, and Max Baer posing in booth No. 32. The walls were decorated with wonderful caricatures, giving the room a sense of community among Hollywood personalities.

HOLLYWOOD BROWN DERBY, 1948. The Brown Derbies were places where celebrities could either relax and see old friends or promote a new film or event. In April 1948, Charles Boyer and Ingrid Bergman discuss their latest film, *The Arch of Triumph*, which was directed by Lewis Milestone for United Artists.

THE BROWN DERBY CAR CAFÉ, 1941. The Brown Derby Car Café building was originally a Willard's Chicken Inn Restaurant, which opened in 1929. The Los Feliz Brown Derby was located at 4500 Los Feliz Boulevard. The Brown Derby Car Café was in part owned by film director Cecil B. DeMille and was modernized with air-conditioning and a new kitchen. The Brown Derby Liquor store had the entrance on Hillhurst. The Brown Derby Car Café closed in 1960, and Michael's of Los Feliz took over the premises. In 1992, Michael's closed, and the building was split into the Derby and Louise's Trattoria.

COPACABANA, 1941. Opening night of the Copacabana brought out Hollywood celebrities and their fans. The new nightclub opened in the former La Conga Club at the Hollywood Recreation Center on Vine Street. The Conga closed in August due to the revocation of its liquor license. The small club's interior was decorated with palm trees and booths placed in little patios overlooking a stage designed like a tropical village. By 1944, the Copacabana moved to 1451 North Cahuenga Boulevard.

HOLLYWOOD CANTEEN, 1944. On October 3, 1942, the former Drouet's Harness Shop on Wilcox Avenue opened as the Hollywood Canteen, a nightclub for servicemen who were visiting Hollywood. Bette Davis and John Garfield organized the club, persuading 14 guilds, unions, and studios to donate labor and materials. Each night, 1,200 servicemen in three shifts from 6:00 p.m. to midnight were entertained as Charles Boyer, Dorothy Lamour, and Marlene Dietrich waited tables. Frank Sinatra did a CBS radio show from the Hollywood Canteen, resulting in pandemonium.

SCHWAB'S PHARMACY, 1949. Originally Schwab's Pharmacy was located in downtown Los Angeles. A branch opened at Sunset Boulevard and Crescent Heights in 1929. By the 1940s, owner Leon Schwab opened a soda fountain and later a restaurant, creating a Hollywood hangout where stars could make their own milk shakes. Greta Garbo and Marlene Dietrich bought makeup there. Forced to close in late 1983 because of financial difficulties, Hollywood's most famous drugstore was torn down for a mall.

FLORENTINE GARDENS, 1947. Owner Guido Braccini opened his extravagant Florentine Gardens nightclub on December 28, 1938, at 5955 Hollywood Boulevard. The European "garden" motif was seen in turn-of-the-20th-century powder blue- and gold-interior designs. The Venetian Room was the main attraction. Braccini advertised a European cocktail bar, restaurant, and dance palace. Stars who headlined there include Sophie Tucker and Paul Whiteman. By 1940, the Venetian Room became the Zanzibar Room, an exotic reinvention that suited the 1950s.

TOM BRENEMAN'S, 1949. On April 28, 1949, just before a morning broadcast, entertainer Tom Breneman died of a heart attack. The building that housed his radio show was originally constructed as the Hollywood Recreation Center in 1940 at 1539 North Vine Street. In 1947, Breneman moved into the former Tropics Restaurant building adjacent to the Hollywood Recreation Center, which he later took. After Breneman, Sammy Davis Jr. and investors bought the building and leased it to ABC Radio. By the end of the 1970s, Merv Griffin took over the building and renamed it the Celebrity Theater.

PLAYERS CLUB, 1948. Film director Preston Sturges opened his own restaurant and private club in an old house at 8225 Sunset Boulevard on the Sunset Strip in 1940. The top level had views of the city and was the daily restaurant. The Blue Room was the formal dining room. In 1942, Sturges built the Playroom, a private theatrical club for his friends, which, by 1951, he formally opened as a dinner-theater venue. Sturges sold his restaurant in 1956, and the building reopened as the Imperial Gardens in June 1957.

NICKODELL MELROSE, 1954. Located at 5511 Melrose Avenue adjacent to the old KHJ, Channel 9, television station and Paramount Studios, Nickodell became a Hollywood institution. Originally the restaurant was opened by Nick Slavich as the Melrose Grotto in 1928, and, by 1954, it was known as Nickodell. When casting the Fred Mertz character for *I Love Lucy*, Desi Arnaz met with William Frawley in Nickodell, which closed on November 30, 1993.

MOCAMBO, 1941. Opened on January 3, 1941, by Felix Young and Charles Morrisson, the Mocambo nightclub at 8588 Sunset Boulevard, near the Trocadero Café on the Sunset Strip, was an immediate success. It vied with the Troc for its star-studded popularity. The Mocambo's interior, with its glass enclosure full of dozens of exotic macaws and lesser parrots, was the hit of Hollywood. Men were required to wear jackets and ties, and the women wore elegant evening dresses.

MOCAMBO, 1942. Regular customers Charles Chaplin and his wife, Paulette Goddard, chat here in 1942. Chaplin just finished new music and commentary for the reissue of his 1925 silent *The Gold Rush*. Goddard had just finished appearing in Paramount's *Star Spangled Rhythm*. The Mocambo was a place where Hollywood megastars could feel comfortable and see friends in an exotic and fun atmosphere.

MOCAMBO, 1942. Another Hollywood celebrity couple who were regulars at the Mocambo were Joan Crawford and her third husband, Philip Terry. Crawford had just finished *Reunion in France* at MGM, and Terry had just appeared in *Wake Island* for Paramount. They were newlyweds at the time.

CIRO'S, 1956. In January 1940, Billy Wilkerson opened Ciro's on the former site of Club Seville at 8433 Sunset Boulevard on the Sunset Strip. He brought in George Vernon Russell to design the exterior facade and assigned Tom Douglas to do a "Hollywood Baroque" style inside. The walls were draped in heavy ribbed silk, dyed pale Reseda green, and the ceiling was painted American Beauty red.

CIRO'S, 1958. Darryl F. Zanuck and Lucille Ball exchange pleasantries during an industry party at Ciro's. Zanuck, who was friends with owner Herman Hover, mounted expensive parties at Ciro's. Zanuck liked the club, food, staff, and his friends, who came to Ciro's to relax. Columnists Hedda Hopper and Louella Parsons reported daily the happenings at the club. Herman Hover took over the club in 1944.

CAFÉ TROCADERO, 1937. The Trocadero opened on September 17, 1934, at 8610 Sunset Boulevard, at Sunset Plaza in the former Club La Boheme building, and was owned by Billy Wilkerson. Wilkerson hired motion picture art director Harold Grieve to design the interior into an elegant French café, which was built on two levels with a very large wine cellar and two bars. In January 1935, Greta Garbo visited the Troc the same night as Marlene Dietrich. Stars who partied at the Trocadero include Bing Crosby, Sam Goldwyn, Jean Harlow, and Myrna Loy. The Troc closed on May 13, 1940.

MUSSO AND FRANK GRILL, 1945. A major Hollywood landmark at 6667 Hollywood Boulevard, Musso and Frank Grill continues to be an industry hangout. Original owners John Musso and Frank Toulet opened the restaurant in late 1919. Early regulars included Charles Chaplin, Gloria Swanson, Cecil B. DeMille, John Barrymore, and Douglas Fairbanks. Writers of the 1920s and 1930s that were customers included William Faulkner and F. Scott Fitzgerald.

SARDI'S, 1939. Club owner Eddie Brandstatter opened Sardi's as his newest restaurant in 1932 at 6315 Hollywood Boulevard. Architect Rudolph Schindler designed the decor. The main dining room was divided into two levels. The alcoves along the walls were indirectly lit, and each table had a caricature of a Hollywood star. In 1934, it was reported that Marlene Dietrich loved the chicken hamburger. Tom Breneman broadcasted his show, *Tom Breneman's Breakfast at Sardi's,* from the restaurant.

VILLA CAPRI, 1957. The original Little Villa Capri in 1939 was across the street on the southwest corner of Yucca Street and McCadden Place. At the end of the lease in 1955, owners Pasquale "Patsy" D'Amore and his brother Franklyn purchased a new site at 6735 Yucca Street from the Masquer's Club. D'Amore opened the restaurant in 1957. D'Amore's first partner was Frank Sinatra. The new restaurant's opening was televised on NBC's *America Tonight after Dark*. Sinatra also hosted a live radio show there between 1960 and 1962. The "Rat Pack," Jimmy Durante, Humphrey Bogart, Judy Garland, and Bing Crosby were regulars.

DON THE BEACHCOMBER, 1941. Originally started as an exotic drink bar in 1934, this venue of Donn Beach's specialized in exotic blended drinks with "funny" names, such as Donn's Zombies, Rum Rhapsodies, Shark's Tooth, and Vicious Virgin. After several locations, Donn moved to a themed Polynesian-style building at 1727 McCadden Place in 1937. The interior had real palm trees. Rooms were named Black Hole of Calcutta and the Cannibal Room. Regulars included Joan Crawford, Mary Pickford, Bing Crosby, Marlene Dietrich, and Frank Sinatra.

NICKODELL ARGYLE, 1951. The Argyle location of Nickodell, at 1600 North Argyle Street, serviced the downtown Hollywood clientele. Hollywood civic and professional groups regularly met at the Argyle restaurant. In 1949, the Television Producers Association held meetings on censorship at the restaurant, which closed in the 1980s.

BARNEY'S BEANERY, 1949. Established by John "Barney" Anthony in 1920 as a roadhouse/diner at 8447 Santa Monica Boulevard in West Hollywood, the Beanery catered to railroad workers, service employees, and studio professionals. Throughout the 1930s, Barney's Beanery had a cocktail lounge with entertainers who lured Sunset Strip patrons. In the 1940s, celebrities came in for chili and onion soup, and a decade later artists and reporters hung out there. The 1960s brought the rock crowd, including Sonny and Cher.

TINY NAYLOR'S DRIVE-IN, 1953. This was William (Tiny) Wallace Naylor's first drive-in restaurant in Hollywood when it was opened in 1949 on the northwest corner of La Brea Avenue and Sunset Boulevard. Humphrey Bogart commented on the unique architecture by saying, "It looks like a huge bird about to take off!" Architect Douglas Honnold designed the large winged canopy. The fluorescent lighting could be seen for miles. Customers included Danny Thomas, Natalie Wood, and Lucille Ball.

MICELI'S PIZZERIA, 2007. Miceli's Pizzeria was established in 1949 on Las Palmas Avenue by Carmen and Sylvia Miceli, along with sisters Angie and Millie and brothers Tony and Sammie. Featuring family recipes from Sicily, the restaurant is popular for its "pizza man in the window." The restaurant became a part of Hollywood lore when Carmen purchased the hand-carved furnishings of the nearby Pig 'N Whistle Restaurant in 1953. Celebrities who ate at Miceli's included Pres. John Kennedy, the Beatles, the Lloyd Bridges family, and Marilyn Monroe.

SHELLY'S MANNE-HOLE, 1963. Opened by famed jazz drummer Shelly Manne at 1640 North Cahuenga Boulevard on November 3, 1960, Shelly's created "a showcase for jazz notables," where his own band, Shelly Manne and His Men, could play. When the club first opened, it was named Shelly Manne's Cahuenga Club. Notable jazz musicians who played the club included Stan Kenton, Ray Brown, Milt Jackson, Thelonious Monk, Gabor Szabo, Carmen McRae, Bill Evans, Sergio Mendez, Stan Getz, and Gary Burton. By late 1973, Manne moved his beloved club to a location in the Wilshire District.

WHISKY A GO GO, 1966. Whisky co-owner Elmer Valentine went to France in 1963 and visited a discotheque that had young dancers on platforms. In Los Angeles, he and his partner, Mario Maglieri, used the idea when they opened the Whisky A Go Go on January 11, 1964, in the old West Hollywood Bank of America building on Clark Street and Sunset Boulevard. The opening act was Johnny Rivers, who later recorded the album *Johnny Rivers: Live at the Whisky*. Through the 1960s, acts at the Whisky included Cream, the Doors, the Byrds, Jimi Hendrix, Otis Redding, The Who, and Alice Cooper. In the 1970s and 1980s, Guns 'n Roses, Led Zeppelin, and B. B. King played there as well.

C. C. BROWN'S, 1983. In 1906, Clarence Clifton Brown began a candy business in downtown Los Angeles. It is said that Brown invented hot fudge sauce and created the hot fudge sundae. In 1924, Brown's son Cliff took over the business and opened a branch in Hollywood in the early 1930s. C. C. Brown's was located at 7007 Hollywood Boulevard in the old Hillcrest Cadillac Building across from the Hollywood Roosevelt Hotel. Joan Crawford and Marlon Brando were regulars. In 1963, employee John Schumacher bought the business and continued it until 1996.

Eight

RADIO AND TELEVISION

Film studio moguls considered television a novelty and were reluctant to invest in it. Yet many early television stations inhabited old movie studios in Hollywood. With televisions eventual popularity, some film companies, like Paramount Pictures, set up experimental television stations (KTLA). Others created companies to produce television shows. Throughout the 1940s and 1950s, Hollywood became the West Coast center for radio and television production. By the early 1950s, Hollywood's film, radio, and television businesses were booming with facilities added to existing studios, making Hollywood the center for the entertainment business in the United States and the world.

The CBS/Columbia Square studios formed the West Coast branch of CBS. In the early 1950s, CBS also produced television shows, including the pilot for *I Love Lucy*. Nearby at Sunset Boulevard and Vine Street, NBC built West Coast Studios on the site of the old Lasky-Paramount Studios. NBC added production but in 1963 moved to Burbank. Earle C. Anthony's independent KECA moved often until ABC took over and established it in East Hollywood. KFWB's radio studio, formerly owned by the Warner Brothers, was moved several times, and by 1977 relocated to Argyle and Yucca Streets until it closed in June 2005. KTLA-TV, originally created by Paramount Pictures, moved its operation to the old Warner Sunset Studios.

In 1964, the KTLA license was sold to Golden West Broadcasters, owned by Gene Autry, who sold it in 1988 to Tribune Company. In 2008, Tribune sold the lot to Hudson Capital, which renamed it Sunset Bronson Studios. Cadillac dealer and radio pioneer Don Lee built the first studio in Hollywood solely for television in 1947. CBS radio and television, already located at Columbia Square, built CBS Television City near the Farmers Market in 1952 for production and acquired Republic Studios under the name CBS Studio Center by 1967. ABC moved to the former Vitagraph/Warner East Hollywood Studios in 1948.

CBS/COLUMBIA SQUARE, 1949. Columbia Broadcasting Company (CBS) programming was national with shows originating in New York or Hollywood. At the 6121 Sunset Boulevard studios, tours in 1939 allowed the public to glimpse the facilities. In 1940, radio shows originating from Hollywood starred Jimmy Durante, Garry Moore, Donald O. Connor, and Ginny Simms. On March 8, 1949, the formal dedication of KTTV, a Times-CBS television station, was hosted by Jack Benny. Throughout the years, CBS television news and KNX broadcasted from Gower Street and Sunset Boulevard.

COLUMBIA SQUARE, 1940. Pictured here is the auto court entrance at 6121 Sunset Boulevard, where the public entered the Columbia Square Playhouse. In 1940, CBS radio shows included *Campbell Soup Company Presents* and *Hollywood Hotel* on KNX. At this time, the Brittingham's Radio Center Restaurant became a popular hangout known as the place "Where the Stars of Screen and Radio Meet." The radio version of *Ozzie and Harriett* premiered in 1944 and ran for 10 years. Other shows in the 1940s included *Mike Stokey's Pantomime Quiz* and *Hollywood Startime* with June Haver and Victor Mature.

COLUMBIA SQUARE PLAYHOUSE, 1940. Known as Studio A, the playhouse was used for live audience shows. In October 1951, the pilot television show *I Love Lucy* was produced at Columbia Square. Its great success led to its move to General Service Studios. Texaco sponsored musical shows at the playhouse that included opera singer James Melton in 1946. By 1958, Columbia Square was the home of KNX Radio, KNXT-TV, Channel 2, and Columbia Records Recording Studios, located in the west wing.

NBC Radio City Hollywood, 1949. Built on the site of the old Famous Players Lasky-Paramount Studios, NBC Radio City opened on October 2, 1938, with the *NBC Carnival* starring Charles Boyer. The new building housed eight studios with a three-story office wing on the northeast corner of Sunset Boulevard and Vine Street. The three-story lobby had a curved mural inside portraying "The Genie of Radio," with radio scenes from around the world.

KLAC Radio/Television, 1946. This photograph, taken during the 1946 Hollywood technicians strike, shows pickets in front of 1000 North Cahuenga Boulevard. KMTR Radio was established on the site in the mid-1930s. Designed in California hacienda style, complete with mission bell tower, tiled roof, and wagon wheel patio, the station was sold in March 1946 and became KLAC radio, 570 on the dial. By September, KLAC-TV had been created. Betty White starred in the first show.

KECA RADIO STUDIOS, 1946. KECA was established in 1929 by Earle C. Anthony, who moved the independent radio station to the former Knights of Columbus Building at 1440 North Highland Avenue in the mid-1930s. In 1944, KECA was sold to NBC and, shortly thereafter, to ABC, which added it to its national network as the Los Angeles affiliate. After World War II, KECA and its Hollywood Radio Playhouse produced shows with audience participation. On September 16, 1949, KECA-TV went on the air at a new studio in East Hollywood and on February 1, 1954, KECA became KABC-TV.

KFWB RADIO STUDIOS, 2001. The Warner Brothers Studios established KFWB in March 1925. The letter K indicated all stations west of the Mississippi, and FWB stood for the four Warner brothers (Jack, Harry, Sam, and Albert). The transmitter was moved in 1928 to the roof of the Warner Hollywood Theater. Around 1953, the station was moved to 6419 Hollywood Boulevard and, in 1968, relaunched in an all-news radio format. In 1977, the station moved again to 6230 Yucca Street (pictured here) and moved again in June 2005 to the Wilshire District of Los Angeles.

RCA LAB AND STUDIO, 1942. The Hollywood division of RCA (MFG Company) was opened in 1937 at 1016 North Sycamore Avenue as the distribution center for radio sets, transmitting equipment, experimental laboratories, recording studios, and later screening rooms. The official name of this branch was the RCA Victor Division of the Radio Corporation of America.

KTLA STUDIOS, 1947. Originally created by Paramount Pictures in 1939, Paramount Television's W6XYZ began experimental operations at 5451 Marathon Street, near Paramount Studios. Full-time programming began on January 22, 1947, under the call letters KTLA with Bob Hope as host. KTLA was founded by technician Klaus Landsberg, who helped build the facilities, including the transmitter. The studio size in 1948 was 65 feet by 75 feet by 25 feet, with six cameras. The KTLA motto was, "KTLA sells Hollywood; Hollywood sells the world."

KTLA REMOTE BROADCAST, 1952. Since 1948, KTLA has covered many Hollywood Christmas Lane parades, making the station the most popular in Los Angeles. In 1958, KTLA began the first "Telecopter" news service, reporting on traffic and special events from a helicopter. KTLA programming during the 1950s included *The Spade Cooley Show, Lawrence Welk,* and *Hopalong Cassidy.*

GOLDEN WEST BROADCASTERS, 1973. In 1955, KTLA television had expanded, and the owner, Paramount, purchased the old Warner Brothers Sunset Studios at 5858 Sunset Boulevard and renamed it the Paramount Sunset Studios. Paramount sold the KTLA license to Golden West Broadcasters on May 13, 1964.

TRIBUNE/KTLA STUDIOS, 1997. In 1967, Gene Autry's Golden West Broadcasters purchased the entire 10-acre studio lot from Paramount and in the following year moved their KMPC Radio station there. The lot has 11 sound stages and was a premiere rental studio. On December 17, 1985, the Tribune Company purchased KTLA and continued renting the facilities to independent producers. Television shows produced here include *Divorce Court, Judge Judy, Heroes* (NBC), *Family Feud,* and *Hannah Montana.*

MUTUAL DON LEE BROADCASTING SYSTEM STUDIOS, 1948. Cadillac dealer and radio pioneer Don Lee conceived the first studio built solely for television. Located at 1313 North Vine Street at Fountain Avenue, the new studio, designed by Claude Beelman and Herman Spackler, included 12 studios and special sound proofing. It was dedicated on August 18, 1948. The show windows displayed Lee's Cadillacs.

DON LEE BROADCASTING, 1948. Studio 4 at 1313 North Vine Street is depicted on July 7, 1948, during a live simulcast (radio and television) of *Queen For a Day*, the company's most popular show. Shows broadcast or taped here included *The Joey Bishop Show*, *The Dating Game*, and *The Newlywed Game*, among others. Today the studios are a branch of the Academy of Motion Picture Arts and Sciences.

KHJ/KNXT Studios, 1959. KTSL, Channel 2, changed its call letters into KNXT in November 1951. Located at 1313 North Vine Street, the Don Lee Studios building was the home to KNXT, KHJ-TV, KHJ AM radio, and by 1960 CBS Films. Public Broadcasting's Los Angeles station, KCET, moved into the building in 1964 and stayed until 1971 when it moved to East Hollywood. By 1971, ABC Pictures Corporation opened while Chuck Barris Productions was producing *The Dating Game, Newlywed Game,* and by 1976 *The Gong Show.*

CBS Television City, 1952. Built on the site of Gilmore Field, Television City was once the cutting edge of television production. Architects Pereira and Luckman designed a studio complex with four sound stages (studios 31, 33, 41 and 43). Located at 7800 Beverly Boulevard (Farmers Market site), Television City was host to *Art Linkletter's House Party, The Carol Burnett Show* (1967–1978), *Merv Griffin Show* (1969–1972), *The Price Is Right* (1972), *The Young and the Restless* (1973), *All In the Family* (1971–1983), *Three's Company* (1977–1984), and *Wheel of Fortune* (1989–1995).

ABC TELEVISION CENTER, 1965. American Broadcasting Company's television station, KECA-TV, purchased the former Vitagraph/Warner Brothers East Hollywood Annex Studio at 4151 Prospect Avenue (at Talmadge Street) in 1948. After remodeling facilities that were established in 1915, KECA-TV, Channel 7, went on the air on September 16, 1949, at the newly named ABC Television Center. An early show produced there was *Space Patrol* (1950–1955). In 1996, ABC was absorbed by the Walt Disney Company, and the lot was renamed the Prospect Studios.

ABC TELEVISION CENTER, 1950. One of the early KECA-TV productions was *The Ruggles*, starring Charlie Ruggles (center seated), Irene Tedrow, Erin O'Brien Moore, Margaret Kerry, Tom Bernard, and Judy Nugent. In 1949, ABC renovated and modernized sound stages at ABC Television Center, and they are still functioning today. Popular shows made at the studio include *American Bandstand* (1957–1987), *The Lawrence Welk Show* (1955–1971), *Let's Make a Deal* (1968–1976), *General Hospital* (1963–1977, Studio D), *The Shield* (2007), and *Grey's Anatomy* (2007).

KTTV-11 METROMEDIA SQUARE, 1979. Located at 5746 Sunset Boulevard on the southeast corner of Van Ness Avenue, KTTV, Channel 11, began operations in 1950 at the Nassour Studio, created by the *Los Angeles Times* and CBS. By April, the station created *Hollywood Television Theater,* and its debut broadcast was a production of Henrik Ibsen's *A Doll's House.* By 1957, KTTV productions included *Sheriff John* and *George Putnam and the News.* In 1963, the Times-Mirror Company sold KTTV to Metromedia Corporation. In 1986, News Corporation of America (Fox) purchased KTTV. In 2000, the studio was sold to Los Angeles Unified School District, and the site became a school in 2008.

KCOP-TV, 1965. Channel 13 went on the air on September 17, 1948, as KMTR-TV and shortly thereafter changed its call letters to KLAC-TV. Betty White was one of the station's early stars. In 1954, the Copley Press purchased KLAC and changed its call letters to KCOP. Several years later, the NAFI Corporation, which would later merge with Chris-Craft Industries, purchased Channel 13 and moved the station to 915 North La Brea Avenue in 1961. In 1995, Chris-Craft partnered with Paramount Pictures, forming the UPN Network (United Paramount Network), and KCOP became the network's Los Angeles station. In 2001, KCOP was sold to the News Corporation (Fox), and KCOP was moved to the Fox TV Center in West Los Angeles.

Nine

THEATERS

During the 1940s, several Hollywood theaters were completely remodeled and became unrecognizable to residents. Exteriors and interiors used new architectural styles, such as streamline moderne and Skouras, a "Hollywood Baroque" design developed by Fox West Coast Theatres president Charles Skouras.

Grauman's Egyptian and Chinese were built as "movie palaces," designed for premieres. The Egyptian, built in 1922, continued as a first-run premiere house well into the 1960s. *Duel in the Sun* (1946) and *Ben-Hur* (1959) premiered at the Egyptian. By the 1970s, this United Artists Theater declined and lost its first-run status. The building was damaged in the 1994 earthquake and was restored and reopened as the American Cinematheque. The Paramount Hollywood Theater (originally known as El Capitan) opened as a film theater in 1941, then it was taken over by Paramount. It was renamed El Capitan by Disney in the 1980s. The Warner Hollywood was a first-run theater from the 1940s into the 1960s. After Pacific Theaters took it over in the 1960s, the theater fell on hard times and was damaged in the 1994 earthquake and closed. The Pantages Theatre was a concert hall in 1940 and was converted into a legitimate stage in 1977.

The neighborhood theaters included the Hawaii Theater on Hollywood Boulevard, showing foreign and classic films; the Filmarte Theatre on Vine Street, built as Hollywood's first art house in 1928 and renovated as a television studio theater in 1952; the Marquis Theatre, one of West Hollywood's early theaters (built in the 1920s), which became an art house showing international and art films, and was later purchased by the Academy of Motion Picture Arts and Sciences for offices and screenings; and the Vogue Theater, with its streamline moderne architecture, which opened as a specialty house exhibiting first-run, foreign, artistic, horror, and mystery films until it closed in the 1990s.

HAWAII THEATER, 1940. One of the most unusual theaters built in Hollywood was the Hawaii Theater, which opened on May 6, 1940. Designed by Carl G. Moeller and Clarence J. Smalle in a Hawaiian motif, the 1,150-seat theater was among the first to be built with a cantilevered roof. Theater owners Albert Galston and Jay Sutton had the interior designed as a tropical environment reflecting Hawaii as "Magic Isles Across the Pacific." In 1964, the theater was sold to the Salvation Army.

EL CAPITAN THEATER, 1941. The premiere of Orson Welles's landmark film *Citizen Kane* (depicted) was a unique event. The El Capitan, built by Hollywood pioneer Charles E. Toberman, opened at 6838 Hollywood Boulevard as a legitimate theater in 1926. The building was designed by Morgan, Walls, and Clements in the Spanish Baroque Revival design. Interior work was by G. Albert Lansburgh in the East Indian Revival style. In preparation for *Citizen Kane* on May 8, 1941, the theater was wired for sound for the first time.

PARAMOUNT HOLLYWOOD, 1942. After the long run of *Citizen Kane* at the El Capitan, Paramount Pictures took over the theater and renamed it the Paramount Hollywood Theater. After a remodeling of the exterior marquee, Cecil B. DeMille's *Reap the Wild Wind* premiered on March 19, 1942. The wartime premiere had no spotlights due to blackout rules, and proceeds went to the U.S. Navy Relief Fund. In 1968, the theater became the Loew's Hollywood Theater until the late 1980s, when Disney restored the building and theater and renamed it El Capitan Theater again.

FILMARTE, 1946. Hollywood's first art house, located at 1228 North Vine Street at La Mirada Street, opened in 1928, screening foreign and silent films. A unit of the West Coast Theaters chain, the Filmarte was programmed by Regge Doran, artistic director. The Swedish film, *The Golden Clown*, was the inaugural show on May 19. Through the 1930s, the venue presented Russian, Swedish, French, and Italian films with some American silents. By 1952, it was remodeled into a television studio theater. In June 1962, *The Steve Allen Show* premiered there.

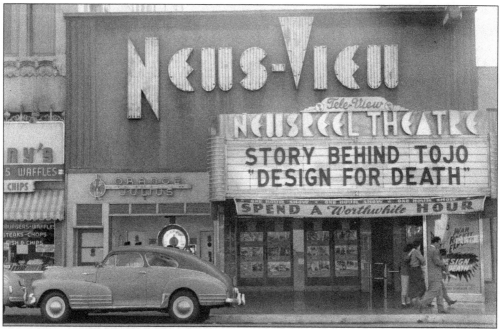

NEWS-VIEW, 1944. The Tele-View Newsreel Theatre/News-View, located at 6656 Hollywood Boulevard, opened on May 2, 1940. The theater was designed by S. Tilden Norton and Frederick Wallis with art deco–lettering as the dominant exterior architectural design. The interior streamline moderne styling used wall murals depicting transportation and aviation progress. By 1944, the building was owned by ABC Theatres, and it closed in the mid-1950s. In 1968, Pacific Theaters acquired and renamed it the Pacific New View.

GUILD, 1951. Originally opened as the Music Box at 6126 Hollywood Boulevard, this theater was renamed the Guild Theatre in 1945 and was refurbished into both a legitimate stage and movie house. NBC acquired it in November 1951, and by 1954, it was remodeled into the Fox Hollywood. By 1960, it was the Pix Hollywood Theater. In 1985, the theater was returned to a legitimate stage and dedicated to Henry Fonda. In 2005, the theater was renamed the Music Box Theatre.

FAIRFAX THEATRE, 1943. Construction began in October 1929 on this theater at Fairfax Avenue and Beverly Boulevard, which was a one-floor house with no balconies and seated 1,500. Designed by W. C. Pennell, the art deco venue hosted Sunday symphony concerts, various studio previews, and, by the 1940s, Max Reinhardt's entertainment industry workshops on the theater's stage.

LOS FELIZ, 1995. Clifford A. Balch designed this neighborhood theater in the art deco style at 1822–1826 North Vermont Avenue, just south of Los Feliz Boulevard. The theater became a unit of the Laemmle circuit, then an art house.

STUDIO, 1948. Opened as an art house in early 1945, the Studio's policy was to show foreign films, including the April exhibition of Los Angeles's first Surrealistic Film Festival. Russian, French, and English films were presented, including Noel Coward's *Brief Encounter*, Alexander Korda's features such as *The Thief of Bagdad*, Jean Cocteau's *The Beauty and the Beast*, and Laurence Olivier's *Henry V* and *Hamlet*. The Studio closed in 1960.

WARNERS HOLLYWOOD, 1949. Originally opened in 1927 as a flagship, Warner Theater, this four-story Italian Renaissance Revival building, was designed by architect G. Albert Lansburgh and was located at 6433 Hollywood Boulevard at Wilcox Avenue. The theater exhibited the Warner classics *Sergeant York*, *They Died With Their Boots On*, and *Casablanca*. On April 29, 1953, *This Is Cinerama* opened to capacity crowds, and the theater continued to show Cinerama films, including *Cinerama Holiday*, *Seven Wonders of the World*, *South Seas Adventure*, *How The West Was Won*, and *Circus World*. In 1965, the theater became a Stanley Warner Theater, and on May 1, 1968, Pacific Theaters bought and renamed it the Hollywood Pacific Theater.

MARQUIS THEATRE, 1945. Located at 9038 Melrose Avenue, east of Doheny Drive, the Marquis was in a neighborhood in Sherman that was later known as West Hollywood. On November 11, 1925, the *Los Angeles Times* announced, "Marquis Theatre opens on Armistice night." The opening film was *The Beautiful Cheat*. On September 20, 1929, the theater was outfitted with Colorart Synchrontone sound systems. On December 22, 1945, Jean Hersholt arranged for the Academy of Motion Picture Arts and Sciences to acquire the theater, who later renamed it the Academy Theater.

HOLLYWOOD PALLADIUM, 1944. The Hollywood Palladium ballroom was built by Norman Chandler, the publisher of the *Los Angeles Times*. The dinner and dancing venue opened on October 31, 1940, as the Hollywood Palladium Ballroom Café with Tommy Dorsey and vocalist Frank Sinatra. Throughout the 1940s, the best dance bands played there, including Harry James, Gene Krupa, Les Brown, Tex Beneke, and Benny Goodman, making the Palladium world famous. By 1961, *The Lawrence Welk Show* aired live on television from the Palladium. The Palladium celebrated its 50th anniversary in 1990. It was restored in 2008 and reopened as a rock music venue.

ESQUIRE, 1946. Located at 419 North Fairfax Avenue in the Fairfax District, the Esquire opened on May 27, 1937, as an art house, showcasing foreign films and later retrospectives featuring Marlene Dietrich and Greta Garbo. Films shown in the 1950s included *The Perfect Woman* and the Yiddish *Catskill Honeymoon*. In 1953, the theater closed and was taken over by Canter's Delicatessen, a landmark in its own right.

IRIS, 1956. After a second remodeling in 1955 (the first was in 1934), the Iris had a new facade, box office, display cases, and 816 seats at 6508 Hollywood Boulevard. More importantly, the theater had a new "Miracle Mirror Screen" adapted for Cinemascope, 3D, VistaVision, and stereophonic sound. It was said that Carol Burnett worked there as a cashier around 1949.

EL CAPITAN NBC-TV, 1952. Originally opened in 1927 as the Hollywood Playhouse, this theater was leased to NBC for *Ken Murray's Blackouts*, a live show in 1942. In 1952, the theater was again leased to NBC, which presented *The Bob Hope Chesterfield Special* as its first televised show there. Other shows followed, including *This is Your Life* and *Truth or Consequences*. In 1963, ABC leased the venue for *The Jerry Lewis Show*, and by 1964, ABC renovated the theater for their *Hollywood Palace* television variety show.

GRAUMAN'S CHINESE THEATRE, 1956. *The Robe* was the first Cinemascope release, premiering in September 1956 with a spectacular neon marquee that lit up Hollywood Boulevard. The theater was remodeled to add the Cinemascope technology, special seating, and sound equipment. On June 5, 1968, Grauman's Chinese Theatre was designated as Los Angeles Historic Cultural Monument No. 55.

GRAUMAN'S CHINESE FORECOURT, 1946. Sid Grauman started the footprint ceremonies in April 1927 for publicity purposes. The ceremonies benefited the theater, star, studio, and the film playing in the theater. Here Sid Grauman places John Barrymore's "Great Profile" into the cement for posterity. Grauman and his theater foreman created a special formula of cement, which was cleaner and stronger than regular cement, so that precise impressions of hands and feet could be left for posterity.

GRAUMAN'S CHINESE FORECOURT, 1965. Sid Grauman's tradition continued with Debbie Reynolds's hands and footprints becoming a part of Hollywood history. Debbie became the 148th film celebrity to be honored with the forecourt ceremony.

VOGUE, 1957. The Vogue was designed by S. Charles Lee in the streamline art moderne style with an American Colonial interior decor. Located at 6675 Hollywood Boulevard, the theater opened on July 9, 1935, with the premiere of *Ladies Crave Excitement*. Throughout the 1930s and 1940s, the Vogue had a varied programming schedule with foreign, American, horror, mystery, and Disney films.

HUNTINGTON HARTFORD, 1958. Originally opened in 1927 as the Vine Street Theater, a legitimate stage, this landmark was, by 1933, known as the Mirror Theater and showed films. It was later renamed the Studio Theater and, during the 1940s, became the CBS Radio Playhouse, a venue for live radio shows. Cecil B. DeMille produced the Lux Radio Theater there and shared the theater with other CBS shows until 1954, when the building was taken over by art patron Huntington Hartford.

JAMES A. DOOLITTLE, 1998. In June 1984, the Huntington Hartford Theatre was up for sale at 1615 North Vine Street. Shortly thereafter, Huntington Hartford Theatre owner James A. Doolittle sold a major interest in the theater to the Center Theater Group and UCLA. By November 1985, the theater reopened as the James A. Doolittle Theater. The Doolittle was bought by the Ricardo Montalban Nosotros Foundation, which converted it to a Latino-oriented venue.

RICARDO MONTALBAN, 2004. In 2002, the Ricardo Montalban Nosotros Foundation renovated the former Doolittle theater, restoring the original exterior architectural design. On May 8, 2004, the building was dedicated as the Ricardo Montalban Theatre.

CINERAMA, 1963. In 1962, Stanley Kramer, the producer of *It's a Mad, Mad, Mad, Mad World*, and the principals behind the wide-screen Cinerama process agreed to premiere the film at a new Hollywood development involving Pacific Theaters and the City of Los Angeles Community Redevelopment Agency. The theater's premiere was on November 3, 1963. The theater's architect was the Welton Beckett Company, which followed the design of Buckminster Fuller's geodesic dome. There are 316 concrete hexagons and pentagons, each weighing 3,200 pounds, bolted together to create this unique theater.

VISTA, 1952. Opened originally in 1923 as the Bard's Hollywood Theatre, this venue was renamed the Vista in 1927. An important neighborhood theater in East Hollywood, located at 4473 Sunset Boulevard at the Hillhurst, Sunset, and Hollywood Boulevard nexus, the Vista was designed by Lewis A. Smith in the Spanish mission style with an Egyptian interior and 700 seats.

VISTA, 2005. In 1985, this theater was remodeled and restored with 70-mm capabilities and surround sound technology to play first-run films. By 1999, the theater was restored again, adding extra Egyptian details. In 2000, the first Silver Lake Film Festival used the theater as the primary venue. The site was once the back lot of the D. W. Griffith Studio, where the sets for the epic film *Intolerance* once stood in 1916.

IVAR, 2003. Built by Armenian restaurant owner Yeghishe Harout in 1951, the Ivar debuted with a production *The Barretts of Wimpole Street*. In 1956, *The Lonely Ship* played there, starring Yiddish actor Maurice Schwartz. Plays such as *The Odd Couple* and *You're a Good Man, Charlie Brown* were presented, but, by 1974, the theater turned into an X-rated film and nude-dancing theater. In 1991, the Inner-city Cultural Center purchased the building, and in 2000, the California Youth Theatre bought the property.

PANTAGES, 2002. Located at 6233 Hollywood Boulevard since 1930, the Pantages with its grand "Hollywood Deco" exterior and interior, is one of Hollywood's great landmarks. In 1949, Howard Hughes bought the theater and named it the RKO-Pantages Theatre. The Academy Awards were held there from 1950 to 1959. In 1977, the Nederlander Group purchased the Pantages and transformed it into a legitimate theater, reopening with *Bubbling Brown Sugar*.

KALEIDOSCOPE, 1968. A concert promotion and film festival exhibition company, Kaleidoscope took over the old Moulin Rouge Theater in March 1968. Kaleidoscope personnel Gary Essert, Skip Taylor, John Hartman, Dick Priest, Hylan Slobodkin, and Marc Wanamaker began to restore the building. Repairs and upgrades of the stage equipment and lighting created a "total environment entertainment" music theater. The first acts to play the theater included Jefferson Airplane, Buffalo Springfield, and Canned Heat.

NICKELODEON ON SUNSET, 2001. Known as the Aquarius Theatre, a legitimate venue since 1968, the Nickelodeon was modified into a television studio theater by the namesake television channel. Nickelodeon productions on the West Coast, originating from the "Nick On Sunset Studio," have included *All That!* and *Dance on Sunset*. In 1978, the Center Theatre Group purchased the Aquarius and continued its production of *Zoot Suit* there until 1979. The Sunset Gower Independent Studios leased it in 1986 to the *Star Search* company. In 1993, the theater was renamed the Chevy Chase Theatre; and in 2001, Nickelodeon bought it.

HOLLYWOOD BOWL, 1940. Laraine Day and Mary Howard, MGM stars, visit the Hollywood Bowl for publicity purposes, helping the Hollywood Chamber of Commerce sell the idea of Hollywood. During the summer season, the "Symphony Under the Stars" series is conducted at the Hollywood Bowl by the Los Angeles Philharmonic. Located at 2301 North Highland Avenue, the Hollywood Bowl is owned by the County of Los Angeles. With a seating capacity of 17,376, the Hollywood Bowl has hosted some of the greatest performers in the world, including the Beatles in 1964 and 1965.

Ten

HOLLYWOOD
REDEVELOPMENT

Development in Hollywood since 2000 has boomed with housing and commercial buildings planned as mixed-use projects, with office, hotel, retail, and housing all in one. The envisioned "city-village" brings more density to Hollywood but with expected quality-of-life improvements.

In 2008, more than 50 ongoing projects in Hollywood are expected to keep alterations coming. Unfortunate events as well changed the Hollywood landscape, such as the fire that gutted the historic Little Country Church of Hollywood, resulting in its demolition. Hollywood Heritage Museum has been working with all agencies of the City and County of Los Angeles to mitigate unforeseen problems and suggest ways of preserving historic landmarks.

The Hollywood Professional Building at 7046 Hollywood Boulevard, a casualty of the 1994 Northridge earthquake, reopened in 2008 as a residential building. Projected developments are expected to encompass Yamashiro and Magic Castle in the Hollywood Hills, which on March 20, 2008, were approved by the Los Angeles Cultural Heritage Commission for cultural landmark status. The property was put up for sale, and Robert Nudelman of Hollywood Heritage Museum was involved in efforts to preserve original elements of the property. During the pending 2008 sale of The Lot, the Pickford-Fairbanks/Samuel Goldwyn Studio in West Hollywood, Nudelman worked with new owners to preserve the original structures.

The Kress/Frederick's Building, constructed in 1934, was recently restored, including the famous neon sign on its art deco roof. Nudelman worked with the new owners to preserve the building's beauty. In August 2008, the Hollywood Palladium renovation moved forward as a public-private partnership with the involvement of the Community Redevelopment Agency and Nudelman. The ongoing renovation and restoration of the Conway Tearle House/American Society of Cinematographers Headquarters and Club House involved Nudelman. One of Hollywood's earliest historic landmarks (1904), the ASC home, is seen in images taken from the Yamashiro site as early as 1910 (before the Yamashiro existed). The property plan is to preserve and restore the house and build nearby a modern ASC headquarters.

In May 2008, Robert Nudelman passed away, leaving many unfinished development projects without his expert historical supervision. Nudelman was Hollywood Heritage's preservation director and became the heart and soul of Hollywood preservation. It is now up to Hollywood Heritage Museum to continue its efforts in working with the City and County of Los Angeles and developers when it comes to the revitalization of Hollywood.

HOLLYWOOD AND VINE STREET, 1994. A northwest view from left to right depicts the Plaza Hotel, Broadway Hollywood, Taft Building, Equitable Building, and the Capitol Records circular tower. Hollywood had undergone some development between the 1950s and 1960s, leaving Hollywood and Vine Street untouched and in disrepair. The large parking lot in the foreground was formerly the site of the Hollywood Brown Derby.

HOLLYWOOD BOULEVARD AT EDGEMONT, 1994. This building on the northwest corner in the 4900 block of Hollywood Boulevard was badly damaged in the Northridge earthquake of 1994. It seemed that the more devastating quake damage occurred east of Western Avenue.

HOLLYWOOD BROWN DERBY BUILDING, 1993. The Vine Street Brown Derby, which was listed on the National Register of Historic Places, closed on April 4, 1985, as the result of a dispute between the Derby's owner, Walter Scharfe, and the new landlords, who recently purchased the property from the Cecil B. DeMille estate. A fire damaged the building in 1987. On January 24, 1994, the Vine Street Brown Derby was demolished after further damage by the Northridge earthquake.

TAV CELEBRITY THEATER, 1994. The old Hollywood Recreational Center and Bowling Alley was vacated in 1993. By 1994, the building had suffered several fires. Merv Griffin had purchased almost the entire block on the west side of Vine Street for his Celebrity Theater and production company in the late 1970s. By 1996, there was one more devastating fire, collapsing the roof and adding to Hollywood's 1990s blight.

HOLLYWOOD PALLADIUM, 2001. In 1961, the Palladium was still a popular venue; Pres. John F. Kennedy spoke at a Democratic fund-raising dinner and Lawrence Welk started a new television series on December 29. The 1970s brought punk rock and other music to the Hollywood Palladium, resulting in rioting and general vandalism of the building. In 1990, the Palladium celebrated its 50th anniversary with a new renovation and future bookings.

FLORENTINE GARDENS, 2002. An important destination for servicemen on leave in Hollywood in the 1940s, this venue increased in popularity in the 1950s with its floor shows and bar scene. It survived by catering to a younger dance crowd. In 1986, the Community Redevelopment Agency voted to designate the Florentine Gardens as a Hollywood historic landmark. On September 13, 2003, the club celebrated its 64th anniversary. In 2004, the City of Los Angeles planned to demolish it for a new fire station. Through the efforts of Hollywood Heritage Museum, the building was preserved.

AVALON, 2002. In 1963, ABC-TV took over this theater for *The Jerry Lewis Show* and continued there with *Hollywood Palace* beginning in 1964. From 1972 to 1976, *The Merv Griffin Show* was in the building. In 1978, the Hollywood Palace Theatre was sold and renamed the Palace. It reopened on October 29, 1982. Such acts as Tina Turner, Huey Lewis, and Fine Young Cannibals performed on the stage. In 2003, the theater reopened as the Avalon for concerts only.

HILLVIEW APARTMENTS, 2005. Built before World War I, the Hillview was restored and opened in 2005 as part of the revitalization of Hollywood Boulevard. Built in 1917 by moguls Jesse Lasky and Samuel Goldwyn to house actors, the structure located on the Hudson Avenue corner was home to silent actresses Mae Busch, Joan Blondell, and Viola Dana. Reborn as "The Pink Lady," the Hillview was badly damaged in the 1994 earthquake prior to restoration.

SUNSET BOULEVARD AND VINE STREET, 2004. November 14, 2003, marked the opening of the first phase of Bond Capitol and former NBA star Earvin "Magic" Johnson's Canyon-Johnson Urban Fund's residential and retail project at the northwest corner of Sunset Boulevard and Vine Street. The site was once home to Wallich's Music City, American Broadcasting Company, and Merv Grifffin Theater.

SUNSET BOULEVARD AND VINE STREET FACADE, 2004. The key element of the development is the 1935 streamline moderne facade that originally opened as the Hollywood Recreation Center and Bowling Alley and is now incorporated on the Vine Street side. Thanks to Hollywood Heritage Museum and Robert Nudelman, the original architectural details were preserved within this development. By 2005, the Bond-Canyon-Johnson companies sold the development to a realty company.

KODAK THEATRE, 2002. The $94-million, 3,400-seat Kodak Theatre formally opened with the 74th Academy Awards on March 24, 2002. Designed by architect David Rockwell, the theater would be the new home of the Academy Awards and Governors Ballroom. Built on the site of the original Hollywood Hotel, the theater was incorporated into a major entertainment and retail center, the Hollywood Highland Project, which was completed in November 2001.

Visit us at
arcadiapublishing.com

CPSIA information can be obtained
at www.ICGtesting.com
Printed in the USA
BVHW010203091019
560619BV00010B/37/P